PAWLEYS ISLAND
An Old Man's Love Story

Robert (Mac) McAlister

PAWLEYS ISLAND: An Old Man's Love Story

Copyright © 2020 by Robert M. McAlister

Published in the United States by
CLASS
Publishing Division
P.O. Box 2884
Pawleys Island, SC 29585
www.ClassAtPawleys.com

Paperback Edition - 2023
ISBN 978-1-955095-23-5

*Cover Photo: North End of Pawleys Island before 1950.
Bowling Alley and drugstore are on beach side of road.
Courtesy of Georgetown County Digital Library.*

All photography restoration by Anne Swift Malarich.

Dedicated to
Mary Shower McAlister and Charlie McAlister

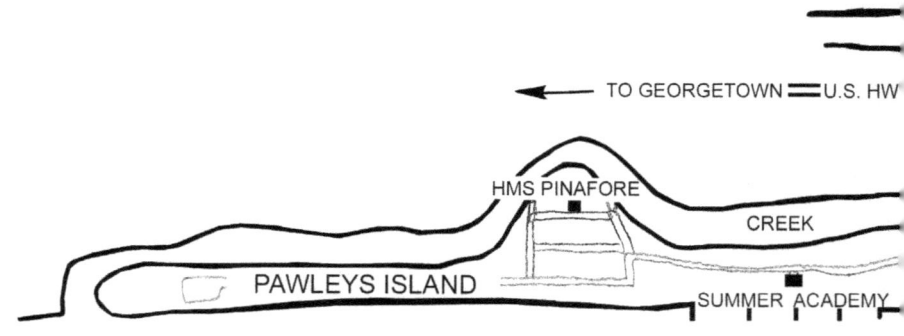

Mac's Map of Pawleys Island

Acknowledgments
Images courtesy of
Georgetown County Digital Library
and Pawleys Island Civic Association

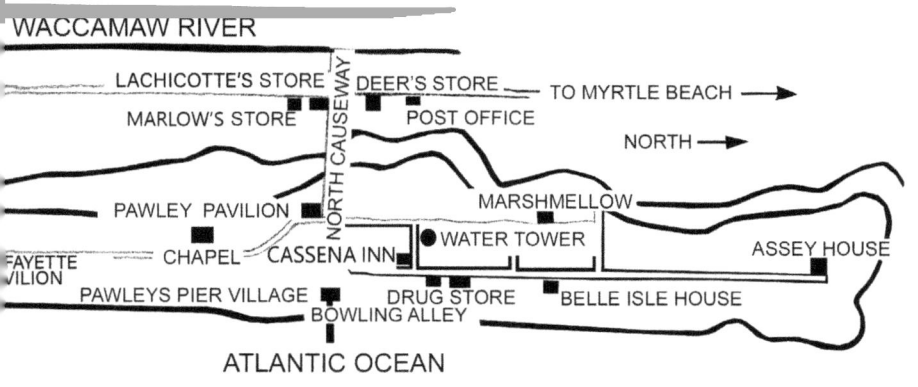

WACCAMAW RIVER
LACHICOTTE'S STORE
MARLOW'S STORE
NORTH CAUSEWAY
DEER'S STORE
POST OFFICE
TO MYRTLE BEACH →
NORTH →
PAWLEY PAVILION
FAYETTE VILION
CHAPEL
CASSENA INN
MARSHMELLOW
WATER TOWER
ASSEY HOUSE
PAWLEYS PIER VILLAGE
BOWLING ALLEY
DRUG STORE
BELLE ISLE HOUSE
ATLANTIC OCEAN

Table of Contents

Introduction

What is it about Pawleys Island, South Carolina, that brings people back, year after year? I'm in my eighties and I've visited the beach at Pawleys Island for almost seventy years, but I still can't say what the fascination is. The closest thing I've found to an answer was told by Dr. Robert E. Quinn in a 1969 article in *South Carolina Magazine*, which said,

"Initially, the knowledge of what it is that makes Pawleys Island the place of lifelong pleasant dreams was non-specific. It was the elusive feeling that something had been lost here and yet might be found again.

"The answer, then, to my dilemma was simple. I, and my fellow lotus-eaters, returned to our lotus patch annually because for all of us Pawleys Island is a repository of the past. We come each year to search for something that is indeed lost – our youth."

Chapter 1
Before My Time, 1700-1950

South End Sketch of Pawleys Island,1848

For those who don't know about Pawleys Island, let me explain that it is located about seventy miles north of Charleston, South Carolina, about twenty-five miles south of Myrtle Beach, with the closest town being the port of Georgetown, about twelve miles farther south. It is technically a barrier island, separated from the mainland by salt marshes and a tidal creek, just a few yards wide. The island is less than four miles long and a quarter mile wide, with a sandy beach running its entire length.

In early times before people built houses on Pawleys Island, sand dunes more than fifty feet high ran along the middle of the island. A few remain. At the edge of the surf, between low and high tides, gently sloping wet gray sand lies smooth, flat and hard. Where there is more slope to the beach, closely spaced ripples of mottled sand stand parallel to the breaking waves. Depending on wind velocity and direction, foam, broken shells, and flotsam and jetsam wash in with the breaking surf and blow along the beach or rest in the sand. Spent waves leave a line in the sand before sliding back to sea under approaching waves. The constant song of surf changes tempo as winds and tides change. Above the high tide line, dry loose sand is white and fine, up to the base of the dunes. Sea oats and viney plants grow on the dune slopes. Stunted trees and bushes of a maritime forest grow thick behind the dunes.

Pawleys Island was named for Percivell Pawley, who claimed property on the island during the early 1700s and is mentioned in the Family Bible.

"Thursday the 14th of November 1723 my father Percivell Pawley drownded at ye North Inlate about 9 or 10 a Clock at nite – being 50 years old & was very harty & healthy."

During the 1600s, some dissatisfied members of wealthy English gentry families immigrated to South Carolina to seek their fortunes. A few obtained land grants of tens of thousands of acres of Low Country land. They took that land away from Native Americans who had been living there for centuries, and they imported slaves from Africa to clear swamps and build rice and indigo plantations along the Waccamaw, Pee Dee, Santee, and Black Rivers. The planters became extremely wealthy, and each summer left their swampy plantations to avoid the threat of "marsh miasma." Their slaves built simple but substantial wooden houses on Pawleys Island, a few of which still exist, and the planters and their families and house slaves lived lives of ease on Pawleys Island until the cooler weather of Fall. Pawleys Island has been a residential summer resort since before the American Revolution.

After the Civil War, planters no longer had slave labor and most of them went out of business. The summer houses on Pawleys Island and elsewhere were uncared for and fell into disrepair. Some of the plantation houses along the nearby rivers were eventually bought by wealthy Northerners and restored as hunting lodges. A few old Pawleys Island summer houses were bought by local residents and remained "arrogantly shabby."

About 1900, some lumber mill investors from the Northeast decided to build the largest lumber mill east of the Mississippi River in Georgetown, South Carolina. They hired experienced executives and workers from mills in the Northeast and Midwest, where the supply of pine and other species of trees used for building materials had been exhausted. Atlantic Coast Lumber Company and other smaller mills bought thousands of acres of land or stumpage all over South Carolina. The trees were milled into lumber, beams, shingles and other wood products and shipped to the big city markets of the Northeast. The imported labor, particularly the executives were enticed to live in this part of the rural South by being offered new houses along the beaches of Pawleys Island or rooms in an existing hotel, now The Pelican Inn.

Transportation between the lumber mills of Georgetown and the beach at Pawleys Island was provided by a steamboat, the *Governor Safford*, which Atlantic Coast Lumber Company had purchased in Florida. The steamboat would leave a wharf along Front Street in Georgetown and steam up the Waccamaw River to Hagley Landing on the mainland opposite Pawleys Island. There, passengers would disembark and board a steam train, which carried passengers along what would become the South Causeway, cross the creek and terminate near the ocean on Pawleys Island. The Atlantic Coast Lumber Company built the railroad bed and tracks, and imported a steam engine and passenger cars from a Coney Island, New York train. This service began in 1900 but ended in 1906, when a storm washed away part of the railroad bed. From then on, transportation between Hagley Landing and the beach at Pawleys Island was provided by horse drawn carriages or carts. The *Governor Safford* steamboat was sold by Atlantic Coast Lumber Company and transportation between Georgetown and Pawleys Island was provided by the steamer *Comanche* and other boats. Some employees of the Atlantic Coast Lumber Company continued to live on Pawleys Island until the mill closed in 1931.

For the past two hundred years, families from all over South Carolina and other states have visited Pawleys Island from Spring until Fall to enjoy a relaxing non-commercial beach setting. The number of houses on Pawleys Island has continued to increase each year. The atmosphere of Pawleys Island is still generally described by owners and visitors as "Arrogantly Shabby."

High sand dunes on nineteenth century Pawleys Island

Atlantic Coast Lumber Company employee houses on Pawleys Island, 1902

Governor Safford *steamboat and ACL train at Hagley Landing*

ACL Hotel, Pelican Inn

Chapter 2
The Drugstore & Lafayette Pavilion, 1954

My family moved from Kentucky to Columbia, South Carolina, in 1948. Our first visit to Pawleys Island was in the summer of 1950, when I was sixteen. We rented a house on the beach toward the south end, the Rains Cottage, for two weeks in July. The house was a typical wood frame, asbestos siding structure, not air conditioned, with a basic kitchen, a bathroom, and three bedrooms, with rough second hand furniture and all the dishes and linens that a weekly renter needed. Waste went into a septic tank and drinking water was from a shallow well. I didn't know anybody on Pawleys Island, but that didn't matter because all I wanted to do was fish in the surf, walk on the beach, ride the waves, and dig holes in the sand.

It was during that summer that I first learned to enjoy walking slowly along the beach with my head down, scanning the sand for the most beautiful shell or the most interesting piece of driftwood. I would pick one up and hold it until I found another one more beautiful or interesting. Then, I would discard the one I had and carry the new one until I found another one. I would save the last one of the day for my collection. One day, I crossed the track of a sea turtle that had come ashore the night before, laid her eggs in a hole she had dug at the base of the sand dune and crawled back into the ocean.

At other times, I would wade out beyond a calm surf with my bamboo surf rod and Penn reel, cast a double-hook rig baited with shrimp as far out as I could and wait for a jerk on the line that meant a whiting or a bluefish, unless it was a catfish, a stingaree or a crab stealing my bait. I would stand

Pawley House

Lemon House

1950s Beach House

Ocean View

Arrogantly Shabby

Seining in the Creek

out there for hours, feeling the sun on my back, listening to the roll of the surf and just daydreaming. If I caught a fish big enough to eat, my mother would fry it for dinner. Once, I caught a nice flat pompano, but my father didn't know what it was until after we had thrown it away. By the end of vacation, our family was hooked on Pawleys Island.

In July 1951, we rented the Rains Cottage again. I wanted to play football as a senior at Dreher High School in Columbia that fall and was trying to obey Coach Kalmbach's orders to get in shape before August practices started, so I would get up early every morning, put on my high top football cleats, and run to the end of the island and back. That was how I met Carol Jean, whose family owned the house next door. She introduced herself and we used to lie on towels in the sunny sand, rubbing Coppertone on each other's backs. She was a sexy-looking 15-year-old peroxide blond, mature for her age. She lived year round in Georgetown where her father ran a store. Some afternoons, she would walk over to the Rains Cottage and help my mother shell peas or pick crabs.

Carol Jean invited me to go with her to the Lafayette Pavilion, which was named after the famous French general who, in 1777, first landed in America just a few miles south of Pawleys Island. The big old ramshackle building was set on pilings a few feet above the marsh, near the South Causeway. The wood siding was covered in scrawled graffiti, outside and inside. The inside was one big room, with booths and benches surrounding a dance floor. The rough wooden tables in the booths were carved with initials and dates, as far back as the 1940's. Before the time of that pavilion, there had been other smaller pavilions on the island. A jukebox accepted quarters to play rock'n roll music. Carol Jean had lots of friends there. She would put on her special dancing slippers and take the hand of one of several boys who wanted to dance with her. I watched in amazement as her little flying feet danced the shag. She was the best dancer there. Everybody watched her as she and a skinny local boy with acne and greasy ducktailed hair did complicated movements in time to the rock-and-roll beat. She tried to teach me the steps but I couldn't even learn to do the reverse sugarfoot. When vacation was over, Carol Jean and I ended our little romance, and I went back home to start football practice.

Lafayette Pavilion

Lafayette Pavilion Interior

It was 1954 before I had a chance to spend a whole summer on Pawleys Island. I had finished my sophomore year at Georgia Tech and had found out that International Paper Company's mill in Georgetown hired engineering students for summer work. A Tech fraternity brother, Bill, and I were hired for the summer. Two friends from high school, McConnell, who was studying pre-law at Clemson and Hal, who was taking pre-med at Carolina, had leased the only drugstore[1] on Pawleys Island to run for the summer. It was located on the ocean side of the main road near the north end of the island and was one of the only commercial establishments on the island. My friends agreed to rent a room to me in the back of the store. Their bedrooms were back there, too.

In June, I drove from our house in Columbia to Pawleys Island in my first car, a used black 1949 Ford convertible, whose top was stuck in the "down" position, rain or shine, awaiting a part from Detroit. I turned off Highway 17 at Lachicotte's Store, crossed the North Causeway and turned left onto the island's beach road. At the water tower, I took a jog to the right, then to the left, toward the north end of the island. The drugstore was only about a block north of the Cassena Inn, one of a few boarding houses on the island. As I was parking between the drugstore and King's Bowling Alley, I became aware of a short, wide and extremely heavy man, who proved to be Red King, wrestling another man out of the bowling alley door. Red – his enormous bare feet planted wide apart – had him in a headlock and was threatening to push his face into a large whirling electric fan. They were hollering and fighting and, finally, Red let him go.

"You fat s.o.b., I'll get you," the other guy said, as he limped away. "Whoa, now," Red pointed his pudgy pinky and squinted his beady mean eyes at him. "You don't mess with Red."

I hastily entered the drugstore, a small nondescript concrete block building, and found my friend McConnell behind the counter. Since there were no customers at the time, he showed me to my room in the back. I noticed that the partition separating my room from the main living area didn't go all of the way up to the roof and that there was no lock on the door. There was a saggy double bed with metal springs and a thin mattress but no chest of drawers, no table and no chair. I complained, without effect, to McConnell that I thought my rent payment of fifty dollars for the summer should include a chest of drawers. I moved in, hung some clothes on nails and put the rest in cardboard boxes. The room did have a window, but it looked out

[1] The Pawleys Island drugstore was owned by John T. Campbell, a businessman in Columbia who owned a drugstore near our house, and several other Columbia drugstores. Campbell was also a politician who became mayor of Columbia and South Carolina Secretary of State. I don't know how he happened to own the Pawleys Island drugstore.

at a side wall of the bowling alley, fifteen feet away. During the first night I found out that the noise of pin boys setting up four lanes of duck pins, the sound of "uh-wump, uh-wump, uh-wump, uh-wump, WHAM, Clinkety, Clink, Clink" and "Set um up, Leroy, you no good n......," was so loud that there was no going to bed until the bowling alley closed at 11 PM.

I accepted my fate and began work at the paper mill the following Monday. I picked up Bill, who didn't have a car and who was renting a room in an annex to the Cassena Inn, and we drove to Georgetown and reported for duty. We were assigned to the Bull Gang, cutting weeds outside of a chain link fence surrounding the huge mill.

After a week on the Bull Gang, the foreman read off my name and one other to report to the engineering office for further assignment. We had volunteered to be part of a survey crew to cut the centerline for a new canal to furnish fresh water to the Mill from the Pee Dee River, thirty miles away. Salt water had contaminated the previous source of water to the mill. Bill hadn't volunteered and had been assigned to the mill chemical lab.

The crew, composed of Phil, me, and three strong black men from the paper mill, Kenny Kenlaw, Frank and Pinckney, met every morning at 7:30 at the woodyard shack. We were joined by Jake, the crew chief and instrument man. Jake was an overweight 260 pounds, six foot two, with thinning red hair and freckles. He had quickly told us what was what. "After I got back from killing Germans in World War II, I played semi-pro fullback in Alabama, and I was hell. I was stronger than any man, except my daddy. He lived to be ninety and could lift 300 pounds when he died. You do what I say and we'll get along fine." Jake chewed tobacco and would sometimes spit juice on our shoes.

We all picked our tools for the day from a locked shed, mostly two-edged bush axes, a broad ax, some shovels and other small equipment, and headed for Jake's pick-up truck. We started the first week's work from inside of the pulp mill compound, near where the canal would end.

During the first week of marking the canal centerline, we were still close enough to the town of Georgetown for us white members of the crew to eat lunch at Mrs. King's boarding house, in town. Jake had hired one other white man for the crew, an older sallow fellow named Fender, who was supposed to be an experienced woodsman. He ate with us that first day. Jake,

Phil, Fender and I sat at one end of a long dining room table. At the other end were two prim middle-aged school teachers, who had been regulars at Mrs. King's for years. Big bowls of vegetables, platters of pork chops and pitchers of sweet tea were placed in the middle of the table to be passed around. We traded smiles and nods with the teachers. Without any warning, Fender shouted down toward the teachers' end of the table, "Pass the goddam meat." The teachers drew back in their chairs with shocked looks on their faces. Jake quickly apologized and ordered Fender to follow him out of the room. That was Fender's first and last day on the crew.

It soon became evident that Phil, who had grown up around the woods and swamps of Low Country South Carolina, was the most experienced and talented woodsman on the crew. In fact, Jake taught Phil to set up and use the expensive German transit that he kept in a mahogany box and carefully secured to its tripod every day. At the beginning of the second week, Jake told Phil that he was going to have to go to the out-of-town boss's office the next day, and Phil was to take over the crew and use of the transit. The day that Phil took over, we were entering a forest of big pine trees. After Phil set up the transit and sighted down the line, he realized that the centerline passed right through the middle of a two-foot diameter pine tree. Phil didn't know how to offset around it, so we decided we had to cut it down. Kenny was the best ax man, so he notched the tree and decided where it should fall. It took most of the morning to cut through it and get it ready to fall. Kenny made the final cut and the tree swayed in the right direction, then twisted and started to fall right toward the expensive and irreplaceable German transit. Phil knew that, if the tree hit the transit, his job was over for the summer. He ran toward the instrument, snatched the tripod, and dove to the ground, just as branches raked down his back. Phil saved the transit and his job. We didn't tell Jake what had happened, and he never knew.

At the end of each typical working day Bill and I returned to Pawleys Island via the Whistling Pig Drive-in, where we picked up a couple of beers. Back at the drugstore, I took a much needed shower, picked the latest crop of ticks off my body and sat on the back porch with a cold bottle of Schlitz. Either McConnell or his partner Hal would be on duty in the front of the store and the other one would be off duty. They were very conscientious about running the drugstore and had a regular schedule for relieving each other. The one who was off was responsible for preparing or obtaining a meal for the other one. One meal a day was bought from the Cassena Inn cafeteria and brought back to be eaten at the store. Giblets and rice was a low cost favorite. The other meals were prepared from the soda fountain.

They were very careful to use the cheapest materials they could find for the food and drink that they sold to customers. A weekly trip was made to McKesson and Robbins wholesale distributors in Georgetown to buy skim milk, artificial vanilla ice cream, and the cheapest American cheese, among other supplies. They opened at nine in the morning and closed at nine at night. They were open every day except Sunday. Hal kept the books and was careful to record every transaction. The only outside help they employed was a junior high school black kid, Robert Lee, who came after school to clean up the store and move stock around. Every two days, the "Ice Boy," one of the Altman family, would drive up in a truck and tong two fifty-pound blocks into the drink cooler. The primary customers of the drugstore were teenaged high school and college kids, and mothers with their young children. McConnell and Hal, especially Hal, was very courteous and helpful to their customers, preparing grilled cheese sandwiches and chocolate milk shakes, using the skim milk, cheap vanilla ice cream, artificial chocolate, and perhaps some stale bread. They sold beach balls, floats, sunglasses, postcards, aspirin, band-aids, and an array of cheap beach toys, which they marked up as much as traffic would bear. There were a few regulars who visited almost every day, including Red King's bratty little daughter, who sat on a stool and complained, but there was no way to get rid of her.

As the summer progressed, operations at the drugstore seemed organized and boring but there were chinks in the system. Hal, who was very neat and precise, was trying desperately to date Judge Morrison's daughter, a beautiful and desirable girl, home for the summer from a fashionable girls' school. When she finally agreed to go out with him, Hal was supposed to have the duty at the store and McConnell didn't want to do double duty on a Saturday night, so there was a disagreement, but McConnell finally relented. Another time, McConnell's friend from Columbia, Andy, staggered into the back of the store late one Friday night and passed out in the hammock on the porch. When morning came, you could see that his face was covered with clotted blood from an incident of the previous night. He had picked up two hitchhikers along Highway 17 who wanted to go to the famous whorehouse, Sunset Lodge, in Georgetown. Andy told them to get in, but turned his car toward Pawleys Island, which was in the opposite direction from Sunset Lodge. They became angry and beat him up. Hal was annoyed that Andy had come to the store and passed out, saying it would give the store a bad name.

McConnell had a weakness for alcohol. When he had had more than two beers, his eyes would get as big as dinner plates and he would begin reciting poetry, such as "I stand amid the roar of a surf tormented shore…," and being generally obnoxious. One evening, after McConnell had had a few beers, he spilled ink on the books, as Hal was making an entry. That led to an altercation, but only verbal. Then, there was the time that two of Hal's Kappa Alpha Order fraternity brothers from the University of South Carolina dropped in, unannounced, to spend a Friday night. They went to the Pavilion first, got drunk and returned to the drugstore about one AM. I had installed a latch on my bedroom door, but one of the drunks climbed over the wall of my bedroom, pushed me to one side of the bed and passed out. I would have moved out after that episode, if I had had anywhere else to go.

One frequent visitor to the store was Salters, who was a student at Carolina. His family lived in Georgetown, where his father sold insurance. On one Saturday night, after the store was closed, McConnell and I and our dates were having a bonfire and drinking beer at the far south end of the island, when Salters showed up without a date. He had had quite a bit to drink and, when we kidded him about not having a date, he was insulted and said he would go get one and be right back. Apparently, he walked over to the parking lot, where couples parked to profess their love, and knocked on the car window of a couple he didn't know. When the girl rolled the window down, he suggested to her that she come with him to a nearby party. Her date took offense, got out of his car and punched Salters in the eye. When Salters returned alone to our group, he had the beginnings of a nasty shiner. On another occasion, after a bunch of us had been in the Pavilion until it closed, Salters suggested we go over to Frank's bar at Atlantic Beach, an all-black bar that stayed open much later. Salters declared that his father sold Frank insurance, and we would be greeted as friends. Actually, we were treated well and were able to buy enough booze to complete our drunken night. As we left, someone suggested that we steal the front steps, just for laughs. I'm glad they were well fastened to the building.

The dance music of the 1950s, played on jukeboxes or occasionally by black combos hired by the management to play at Pawleys Island's Lafayette Pavilion, was almost all composed by and played by blacks. Early songs, like "Drinkin' wine, spoodie oodie, drinkin' wine, pop pop" were followed by "Oh, oh oh, yes, I'm the great pretender" and "If your ol' man ain't treaten' you right, come up and see ol' Dan. He'll rock 'em, roll 'em all night long, he's the sixty minute man," and many others. Their rhythm and blues and rock'n roll music was the most popular music of the 50s, even though black people in the South weren't allowed to dance or listen to it in the same social setting as white people. Those were still the days of Jim Crow, where all social facilities were separate for blacks and whites. If a black person visited Pawleys Island, it was usually because that person had been hired by a white person to do some task, whether it be to cook a meal or play a saxophone at the Pavilion. Growing up in the South, I never went to school or had any social contact with a black person until I was out of college. There were rare exceptions to those rules but consequences resulted from breaking them. Black people had their own resort, McKenzie Beach and Atlantic Beach, just north of Pawleys Island. The black people who worked for white people on Pawleys Island lived on the mainland, west of Highway 17, or in the ground floor servants' quarters of one of the beach houses.

Black Ladies, Going Fishing

By mid-July the centerline of the canal had been cleared beyond the dense forests of loblolly pines, which were loaded with ticks and chiggers. We had come to the edge of the swamps of Tupelo Bay and Carvers Bay, where cypress knees poked out from green scum on top of pools of shallow black water. Beyond that, the swamp bottom rose a little and there were no trees, only bushes and thick bullvine. We came across the stinking mash pits of two abandoned white lightning stills. One still had the copper pipes in place but all of that disappeared during the next night. The next day two scruffy barefooted white guys appeared from nowhere and walked through the weeds and thorns toward us. They had no shirts on and needed haircuts and shaves. We stopped working and watched them approach.

One of them said, "What you'all doin here? This is our land, and you all better git off from it." It was hard to believe that anyone could have lived in such a remote and inhospitable swamp. About that time, Phil recognized the other guy. He was a man that Phil's uncle, a deputy sheriff, had arrested the year before for illegally selling fresh water fish. Phil had helped his uncle catch the man. Phil tried to hide his face behind Jake and me, but the man recognized Phil and yelled, "I'm goin to kill you." He lunged toward Phil, but Jake grabbed the stout eight-foot range pole and drew it back. "You come one more step and I'll knock your goddamned head off. Now both of you get the hell out of here and don't come back." They said they would go but would come back the next day with a gun. We all agreed that Phil should be off the crew for at least a few days.[2]

That summer of 1954 was the hottest in my memory. Resting between turns at cutting the canal centerline through thick brush, I wiped sweat out of my eyes and drank lemonade laced with salt out of a big thermos Jake carried. It was mid-afternoon on Friday and time to make the two-mile hike back to the truck. I wished to hell I could think of a way not to have to go back into Carvers Bay for another six weeks.

"Hey, Jake, don't you think you could use another man? It's a lot of cutting for just us. How about my friend Billy in the lab?"

[2]Phil continued to live in the South Carolina Low Country. He became Thomas Yawkey's superintendent and manager of his property on South Island, Cat Island and North Island. He lived on South Island for many years and became a reknowned wildlife photographer and an international expert concerning alligators.

"Hell, no," Jake answered. "I got pride in my crew. You'all are the best goddam bush cutters in South Carolina. We'll be the first humans to cross Carvers Bay since before Columbus. We can do it." Jake balled up his fist and punched the air.

When we got back to town, I picked up my pay envelope at the office, looking in to see if sexy Rene was sitting at her desk. She was and she smiled at me. My heart pounded, but I walked on, too tired and dirty to speak to her. I sat down on the curb outside the gate to wait for Billy. What a girl, I thought. Damn, this job is getting downright depressing. It's too hard, it's dangerous, and I'm too tired at night to make any time with Rene. And Jake's so full of shit. He doesn't do a damn thing but talk. I've got to find a way out of that swamp.

Billy walked up. "Wow, you're filthy. What have you been doing? Don't tell me. I know you've been in the swamp. By the way, I ate lunch with Rene today. Let's go by The Pig and get a beer."

I looked at Billy, clean clothes and fresh as a daisy. How did he get that job, I thought, washing out jars and taking samples. To hear him talk you'd think he was a goddam scientist. I pulled into the parking lot of The Whistling Pig Drive-in. Billy jumped out and ran in to get a six pack. I sat in the car and watched a big rat run out from under the building, dragging the remains of a Bar-B-Que sandwich and disappear into the marsh. As we drove across the Waccamaw River bridge toward Pawleys Island, Billy popped open two beers with a church key.

"How was your week?" Billy asked

"Shitty. I tried to get Jake to put you on the crew to replace me," I laughed.

"To hell with that. I'm needed in the lab. Don't you dare try to get me out in that swamp. I'll kill you first."

"How did you get that job anyway? My grade point average is higher than yours."

"You volunteered to be outdoors. I sacrificed myself to be cooped up all day. It turned out I was just lucky. You want to go to the Pavilion later?"

"Nah, I'm too tired. I'll eat at the cafeteria and go on to bed. I'll see you there tomorrow night." Billy got out at the Cassena Inn.

I had become depressed and desperate to do anything to get relief. I had thought up a possible solution. During that next Monday morning, we had cut into a part of Carvers Bay that was a desolate dry swamp of eight-foot tall brush and vines so thick that nothing could go through until the wall of bush was cut down. As we were putting our lunches and the water keg in the shade at the side of the path, a pair of crows cut across the cloudless sky. Their mournful caws were the only sounds of the swamp.

"Look at them damn crows," Kenny said. "They're sayin 'Caava, Caava." He chuckled to himself, rolling roadmap eyes from a weekend of booze. I picked up his bush ax.

"I'll cut now," I said. I started swinging my ax like a madman at the wall of thick bush, chopping and pulling with unusual enthusiasm. It was a hundred degrees.

"Slow down, man," said Kenny. About that time my bush ax bounced back from a thick vine. The sharp back edge of the blade caught my right hand across the knuckle of my middle finger. Blood spewed out. I dropped the ax.

"Oh, shit, I've cut myself." Jake opened the first aid kit and tried to blot the blood, but it was too wide a cut to stop.

"It looks like you'll need stitches. Can you hold it closed long enough to walk back to the truck? Kenny, you drive him to the doctor." Kenny and I started back along the trail.

"Are you ok?" asked Kenny.

"Yeah, I'll make it. I guess this is my last walk through Carvers Bay. Too bad."

"You didn't do it on purpose, did you?" Kenny grinned. I smiled back at him, gritted my teeth and kept walking. An hour later we were in Dr. Assey's office. He looked at the finger.

"Probably take four stitches. Too late for Novacain to do any good. It won't hurt much."

He sewed it up. When he was finished he said to me, "Now you stay home the rest of today. Tomorrow, you tell your boss to give you an easy inside job for the rest of the summer."

That was my last day in the swamp. Jake took my advice and made Billy replace me.

Business at the drugstore dropped off drastically in August. With nothing much to do, McConnell and Hal hunted for distractions to make life more interesting. They adopted a neurotic stray cat that lived on the concrete floor behind the soda fountain and licked itself all day. McConnell rescued a baby sandpiper from the rising surf and tried to feed it sugar water with an eye dropper, but it died. We occasionally pulled a fifty-foot seine across the tidal pools on the back side of the island, trying to catch enough shrimp for a meal. Once, McConnell and I captured a four-pound flounder in the seine.

I still worked at the paper mill during the day, but in the evenings and on weekends I began to look around me and appreciate the uniqueness of Pawleys Island. I would sit on the back porch of the drugstore and look out to sea. I got up early to watch a red sun peep above the horizon, rise into the sky and make the sand so hot I had to run across to reach the damp cool sand. In the middle of the day I would stand chest deep in the calm ocean swells and feel minnows touching my leg. I watched the sun go down behind the marsh, and the sand was cool under my feet. There were nights when thunderstorms rolled in from the ocean, lightning streaked from cloud to cloud, and thunder booms came closer and closer. Gusts of wind cooled things down just before the hard rain came, pattering the tin roof and pouring down the screen. After the rain there were spatter marks in the loose sand.

One day in early August, McConnell suggested that they should make a billboard, advertising the store. I offered to paint the lettering on a 4x8 piece of plywood and stake it out in the marsh beside the North Causeway. I convinced them that it should be a mysterious quotation in a foreign language that no one could read, with ISLAND DRUG lettered at the bottom, and people would come in to find out what the sign said. We selected the words, "TIMEO DANAOS ET DONA FERENTES – ISLAND DRUG." By the time the sign was up, it was late August. I had to quit work and drive back to Atlanta to start school, so I never knew whether the sign worked. It was blown away, along with almost everything else on Pawleys Island during Hurricane Hazel in October 1954. Hazel temporarily cut the island into three parts and destroyed or damaged many of the houses on the island.

Hurricane Hazel Damage

Hurricane Hazel Damage

Chapter 3
Drugstore Life after Hurricane Hazel, 1955

Having survived working in the swamps for IP in 1954, I was offered a job in the IP engineering office for the summer of 1955. I found out that the Pawleys Island drugstore, which had barely survived Hurricane Hazel, was going to be leased to two USC law students, Billy and Claude. I didn't know them, but I contacted Billy and he agreed to rent the same room to me for the summer. When I arrived, I discovered that the rear half of the drugstore had been undermined by the hurricane. The foundation blocks had partially collapsed and the wood floor slanted about six inches from front to back, but it was livable. The front part of the store was on a concrete slab and, although it had been flooded, it was okay to use. Red King's bowling alley had been flooded and the wooden alleys had buckled, but he opened up anyway. As the duckpin balls rolled down the corrugated alley, they bounced from buckle to buckle, making an even louder noise, but kids came in and bowled anyway. Red was his same old self, standing at the back of the bowling alley, barefooted in his overalls, with no shirt covering his big belly, drinking corn whiskey out of a mason jar and yelling at his pinboys. He had become particularly famous during Hurricane Hazel, reportedly hanging on to a tree branch that floated across the Pawleys Island creek to the mainland and back again when the eye of the storm passed.

I soon discovered that the store was going to be run in a much more casual way than the year before. Billy, a slightly pompous fellow who was called Snerd by some of his friends, and Claude, a friendly guy who was called Senate and whose father was a Judge in Spartanburg, were living on

Pawleys Island to have a good time. They seemed to be well fixed for money to stock the store. They rented a popcorn machine and bought a massive amount of bagged popcorn, only to discover that the machine had a short circuit that caused anyone putting a dime into the slot to receive a severe electrical shock. After a few experiences with little children being knocked to the floor and their angry mothers threatening suit, they disconnected the popcorn machine for the summer. They rented a Wurlitzer jukebox and crammed it into the small space in front of the soda fountain. They stocked it with rock 'n roll records, which proved popular with their adolescent customers.

Senate and Snerd weren't about to sacrifice their vacations to the profit motive. Senate hired Sam, a black high school student to do odd jobs, starting with polishing shoes and later, working behind the counter, much to the disapproval of some lily white customers. Good luck brought two teeny bopper blondes into the store, asking for part time work, sweeping up and closing the store in the evening. In exchange, they received free use of the jukebox and an occasional gift of a pair of sunglasses or a movie magazine. Senate and Snerd decided to open the store at ten or ten thirty and close whenever the girls finished their nightly chores. These hours gave the proprietors enough free time to hit the beach during the day and check out the Pavilion at night. Weekends inevitably brought a crop of visiting KA fraternity brothers, wanting to store their beer in the drugstore cooler or turn up the jukebox volume. As Saturday night approached, Snerd, who had the duty at the soda fountain, would hide his beers behind the counter and soon, a party would begin. Drinking games, dancing, Snerd imitating the singing of Eartha Kitt, giving away sunglasses, you never knew what would be next on a Saturday night. They would close early if a black combo was playing at the Pavilion.

I protected my space in the back but was at the mercy of the weekend crowds. On one drunken Saturday night, after the Pavilion had closed, Senate and some drunken friends returned to the store, discovered a fresh rat in a trap and pretended to cook it on the grill, where cheese sandwiches were grilled during the week. After more laughter, singing and bouncing off the walls, they finally went to bed. I got even with them on Monday morning. I got up before seven because I had to be at work at 7:30. Before I left the store, I rolled the juke box out from the wall, turned the volume all the way up, selected a hit, titled "A'screamin and a'dyin and a'rollin on the floor," pressed the Select button 10 times and headed for Georgetown.

I did my share of weekend Pavilion beer drinking. I had the advantage of knowing some of the young Georgetown crowd, called "The Local Gorillas" by Snerd and his college friends. The Georgetown crowd was generally younger, rowdier, sloppier, and felt like they owned the place. One of the most menacing of the local Georgetown crowd was Howard, who was large, strong, hairy and an apparent leader of the group. Actually, when I got to know him, he turned out to be a very nice fellow and was not nearly as tough as he looked. Another of the local group was Bing, who was a handsome ladies' man. He had his eye on a particular girl he wanted to impress, and he asked me if we could stage a fake fight, in which he would appear the victor and the one to have defended the honor of this girl. I declined the invitation. He must have found some other way of wooing the girl who, I must say, was attractive.

The college crowd had its own dress code: Bermuda shorts, striped dress shirts with buttoned down collars, and penny loafers with no socks. They sat together in booths, awaiting their queen, Betty from Greenville, to show up. They danced the shag and looked properly bored. I wasn't really part of either group.

Boys of both groups had the same idea in mind, which was to make a big enough impression on the girl of their dreams for her to agree to accompany him out the door of the Pavilion, cross the street, and take a well-used path to the beach for some loving. As the night wore on and beer consumption took effect, boys sometimes lowered their expectations concerning the girls of their dreams, but the desire for loving remained.

I got to know Herman and Pat, the young, all-business couple who leased and operated the Pavilion. Herman was a short wiry man who wore glasses and worked as an electrician in the paper mill power plant. Pat was a good looking vivacious brunette. In five seconds, either Herman or Pat could reach behind them, flip open the hinged cover of a long metal cooler full of ice, grab the correct brand of beer can, place it in the counter mounted church key opener, punch open the can, and set it on the counter for the customer. They collected the cash and maintained reasonable order.

Potential troublemakers were ordered out by Herman, and he had a billy club below the counter, just in case. Herman asked me to help him out, behind the counter on Fourth of July weekend, and I did. I think we sold over five hundred, thirty-cent beers in one night. Senate would approach the bar and say, "Gimme a Bud, Mac." After 8 or 10 trips, he would say, "Gimme a Mac, Bud." Pat would announce "last call" at quarter to midnight and sales stopped at midnight. A few extra beers would be sneaked out in paper cups a little after midnight, depending on whether Deputy Altman was around.

After 1954, people who had experienced or been told about Hurricane Hazel, especially Snerd and Senate, were gun shy about what the 1955 hurricane season would bring. As Hurricane Connie formed and threatened the east coast in early August, Snerd and Senate decided to evacuate. They packed most of the stock in their cars, closed the store, left a key with me, and headed toward Senate's home in Spartanburg.

On the morning that the hurricane passed Pawleys Island, far out at sea, two friends, who also worked at the paper mill, and I borrowed raincoats, rain hats and boots from the woodyard shack, snuck out the front gate and drove toward Wilmington, North Carolina, where Hurricane Connie was supposed to come ashore. When we got to the base of the bridge which led over to Wrightsville Beach, the police were stopping all cars because the island had been evacuated. We had to lie, showing the police a Brownie camera and saying we were journalists with the Atlanta Constitution, and they let us onto the island. It was probably blowing fifty knots, with seventy-knot gusts, when we drove up to the Wrightsville Beach pier and parked. The pier was intact but waves were pounding the shore and ripping out the first floors of beach houses. Outside of the entrance to the pier restaurant was a pile of cases of unopened beer, left in the haste of departure. That was where all of the journalists were gathered, helping themselves to free beer. We did the same for a while, until most of the excitement seemed to be over, and we drove back to Georgetown.

Two days later, when the proprietors of the drugstore were sure that the hurricane was no longer a threat, they returned. Just after they reopened, another hurricane, Diane, threatened the coast. They didn't know what to do. Their final decision was to close again, for good. They packed their cars but hung around for one more weekend of vacation. Labor Day was less than two weeks away and they were losing money anyway. Diane missed Pawleys Island, also. I stayed in the back of the store until after Labor Day, helping Herman and Pat during that busy weekend; then, drove back to Atlanta for my senior year at Tech.

After graduation in late May 1956, I drove to Columbia to meet an old friend, Tom, who was graduating from the University of South Carolina. On Friday night, we attended the annual USC German Club Ball, which began at midnight and lasted until 6 AM. It was a wonderful party, with three dance bands alternating through the night. When it was over, Tom and I stopped by an A&P grocery store, bought three cases of extremely cheap Tudor beer and headed for Pawleys Island. We intended to stay for a week, although we didn't have a place to sleep. Tom had a girlfriend who went to Converse College. Some of the girls from this all-girl school in Spartanburg had rented a beach house at Pawleys for a weeklong house party, and Tom figured we could sleep under their house.

Each year, during the first week in June, several fraternities, sororities and other organizations rented houses on Pawleys Island for house parties. Many Pawleys' home owners wouldn't rent to house parties because of potential damage and complaints from neighbors about late nights and loud noises, but several did, and there were usually ten or fifteen house parties going on during that week.

Fortunately, I was introduced to Peggy, a friend of Tom's girlfriend, and we all participated in the First-Week-In-June house party activities of Pawleys Island. We joined a crowd on the beach in the late morning, riding waves and standing in deep water beyond the breakers to keep cool. We lay in the sand and let the sun beat down on our bodies, feeling that we were turning brown, not caring about what the sun was doing to our skin. There was still a little ice in the cooler, and we sampled the first beers of the day. A "church key" was tied to a handle of the cooler. We played stick ball with a solid rubber ball, cut in half. We passed a football back and forth. Somebody's dog dove through the waves to retrieve a tennis ball. The day was hot and we covered our heads with beach towels. We ate cheese and peanut butter crackers and drank beer through the afternoon. My would-be girlfriend and I joined Tommy and his girl for our only splurge of the week, dinner at Rusty Ann's restaurant. I had put on a shirt and shoes for the occasion. Otherwise, they wouldn't have let me in the restaurant. We ate fried shrimp. The girls paid for theirs.

When we had finished dinner, it was time to go to the Pavilion. Cars were lined up, bumper to bumper on both sides of the beach road and along the edge of the South Causeway. We parked and walked along the dark road toward music that blasted from the Lafayette Pavilion. The entrance porch was jammed with sweaty people, who had escaped from the inside and were trying to get a little fresh air. They smoked cigarettes and sucked on cans of beer, preparing to reenter the inside turmoil. We plunged in. There was an African American band in a corner, a saxophone or maybe two saxophones, drums, a piano and an electric guitar. They had been playing hard for a while and sweat was running down their faces. They were wailing out rock and roll beats. Some kids, college or high school, I couldn't tell which, were crowded around the band, jumping up and down and shouting encouragement. The dance floor was jammed with shaggers, trying to look cool but having a hard time avoiding other couples doing the same thing. There was a crowd of kids at the bar, impatiently pushing toward Herman, Pat and two other bartenders, who were opening beers as fast as they could, shoving them at customers and collecting money. The rest of the big room was standing room only, except for a lucky few who sat in booths, guarding their places and stacking tables with empty beer cans. The noise level was terrific, bouncing off the walls, a loud buzz of conversation and laughter, with occasional shouts and shrieks. There was no breeze coming through the open shuttered windows and the temperature inside must have been a hundred degrees. Standing in line, pressed against a wall were girls, trying to look dignified as they waited to enter what was jokingly known as the Ladies' Room. Next to that line was a mob of boys, shoving toward an opening leading into the "Men's Room," a stopped up urinal, an overflowing toilet and a deck overlooking the marsh, where four guys stood side by side, peeing over the side and into the mud, below. The whole inside of the pavilion throbbed to the beat of the music. After a long jam session, the musicians took a break, elbowed their way outside and stood by their truck, passing a pint of whiskey around. Inside, a juke box continued to blare out popular rock tunes and people still danced, chugalugged beers and shouted at each other.

PAWLEYS ISLAND

We jammed the Pavilion each night, dancing and playing Thumper, Lion Tamer and other beer drinking games. The more rambunctious revelers crawled through the rafters or got into fights with the local gorillas and each other. We sat around and listened to stories about old days in the Pavilion, when a drunk was stripped, painted blue and tossed from a window of the Pavilion, into the marsh. And the time two dignified Harvard MBA students contested a parking space in front of the Pavilion with a car full of Marines from Parris Island, and the smallest Marine was sent to throw both students into the marsh. And the story about Pete sitting at one end of the Pavilion bar, minding his own business, while a large bully was threatening his little brother, farther down the bar. Pete snuck up on the guy, drew back and cold cocked him with one punch.

During the days, we baked in the sun and had "get brown" contests. In the late afternoon, we would sit in a circle in the middle of the main road, playing beer drinking games and blocking traffic, until Deputy Altman arrived and made us move away.

One day I went by a University of South Carolina fraternity house party house to look for a person I knew. When I got there in the late afternoon, there were a number of brothers gathered outside, looking up at a person on the roof. I was told that this person was another fraternity brother who was blind and was being vocally directed by the others on how to climb down onto a balcony. I listened to their directions to the blind brother. "Keep your hands where they are. Move your right foot over the edge. No, that's too much. Slide your right foot down until you feel a pipe sticking up. That's it. Now, bring your right hand down where your foot is. Easy now."

"Am I doing ok?" came from the boy on the roof.

"Yes, that's fine. Now slide on down until I tell you to stop."

The conversation went on and on until the blind brother reached the balcony and stood on the deck. Everyone cheered. It was easy to see that they had all been drinking beer all afternoon, including the blind brother. It was all a game. My friend wasn't there so I left.

When that week was over, I said good-bye to Tom and the girls and moved into a landmark Georgetown building, the Pink Elephant, which once may have been a whorehouse, to get ready to report for work. I shared an apartment with a friend, William, and we both worked in the paper mill's engineering office. We knew that this would be our last summer of irresponsibility before facing life in the real world as adults. William had just graduated near the top of his class at West Point and would go on active duty as an Army officer at the end of August. I was facing the draft and had decided to join the Navy for two years, starting in September. The summer dragged along. I went to the Pawleys Island Pavilion on a few Saturday nights, looking for someone new, some perfect girl to fall in love with. One night, I sat in a booth with a friend, drinking a beer, when there was a flutter of excitement at the door and a wedding party from the little church in the middle of the island rushed in. The bridesmaids wore long white dresses and danced barefooted. They were so beautiful. I finally met one of them. She, like the rest of the wedding party, lived in Greenville. She was very pretty, vivacious, with freckles. We danced and drank a beer together. She said I could take her home to her family's beach house. I kissed her goodnight and wanted to get to know her better, but she left for Greenville the next day and I never saw her again. Oh, well, just another Pawleys Island story.

At the end of the summer, Bill left for the Army, and I headed for Navy Boot Camp in Bainbridge, Maryland. I later decided to go to Officer Candidate School. When I graduated, I requested duty in Europe or anywhere overseas. The Navy sent me back to South Carolina, to the Marine Air Station in Beaufort for two years. I still made occasional visits to Pawleys Island during those years, but Savannah and Tybee Beach were closer.

I did spend a week of leave on my friend McConnell's old wooden Chris Craft cabin cruiser, the *Juanita Jane*, which was docked at Panther Johnson's marina, on the Sampit River, near Georgetown.[3] It was a stifling hot summer afternoon in August, 1958, when I parked my car at the end of the sandy washboard road to Panther's marina. Panther was sitting outside, in the shade, shirtless in a broken chair, drinking straight scotch out of a jelly glass. His flushed weather beaten face was turned to catch a little breeze from a slowly whirling fan in front of his marine railway. He was trading sea stories with a couple of other old reprobates, who owned or worked on boats, strung out along the dock or tied up in the rusty tin boathouse. I stopped to listen to a good one about a drunken U.S. Congressman misbehaving with the Madam of Sunset Lodge, Georgetown's world famous house of prostitution. Then, I moved on down the dock to open up and throw my sea bag on board the *Juanita Jane*, letting out smells of mildew and rotting wood.

Soon, McConnell arrived with a big cooler of iced down Schlitz, and we began to plan our vacation, the highlight of which would hopefully be a series of moonlight river cruises with eager and beautiful young women, already lined up. During the day we would sleep and prepare for the next night's cruise. Unfortunately, the first night's guests failed to show up, and we had to drive to Pawleys Island, to the Lafayette Pavilion, to shanghai a crew of college girls for a late night cruise. It was ten PM before the *Juanita Jane* was underway, guided by our drunken captain, singing, "What will we do there? What will we see there? What'll be the big surprise? There may be senoritas with dark and flashing eyes, Hey!" The college girls thought he was hilarious. He pretended to scan the muddy banks of the creek with the powerful mile ray spotlight, looking for wide-spaced, red eye reflections from big alligators. There was much giggling and popping of beer can tops. At a wide place in the creek, McConnell cut off the engine and we drifted, jumping off the roof, swimming around the boat and playing hanky-panky with the girls. All in all, the cruise was a success, even when our captain approached the dock at high speed and ordered the crew to jump off and tie her up. Dock pilings whizzed by, way too fast to jump, and we bounced off a few, before a sudden and final stop. "That's what I get for trusting the lines to a drunk," he disciplined me. The girls, declaring their love for us, The Sea and the *Juanita Jane*, drove away, looking forward to other romantic moonlight cruises. By the end of the week, I'd developed a distinct liking for this kind of cruising life.

[3]Panther Johnson's marina was located on a creek off the Sampit River, where Harmony Development is now. Nothing is left except for a few pilings. Panther (Capt. Johnson) appeared from out of nowhere after WWII on a boat passing through, and stayed for the rest of his life. McConnell and Capt. Johnson had become friends over the years. One summer, after Mary and I were married, McConnell and his date Zo were invited by Capt. Johnson into his little house, next to the marina, an unusual occurrence. The five of us sat around his kitchen table, drinking scotch out of jelly glasses when he asked if we would like to see his wife. He led us to the bedroom and opened the door. We were much taken aback by the sight of a full size inflated plastic woman, lying in the bed. Capt. Johnson laughed at our expressions and closed the door. When Capt. Panther Johnson died a few years later, it was discovered that he was not who he said he was. He had been cashing social security checks made out to someone named Johnson but it wasn't him.

Chapter 4
Building the Pawley Pavilion, 1960

My three years of active duty in the Navy ended in February 1960. After two pleasant weeks of leave in Rio, Brazil, I returned to Georgetown to work for International Paper Company. Still a bachelor, I rented a pink, asbestos-sided house, named HMS *Pinafore*, toward the south end of Pawleys Island. It was located in the fourth row of houses from the beach, which was all I could afford to rent on a year-round basis. The house had no central heat, just one gas space heater. The unheated bathroom, with tub, was in a separate structure, like an outhouse. My closest neighbors were Linwood and Nancy Altman, who lived across the road and owned Lachicotte's Store, and Nancy's sister and her husband. I don't believe there were more than six houses occupied on the whole island that winter.

I came down with a bad case of the flu right away. It was so bad that I drove to the northernmost house on the island[4] to see Dr. Philip Assey, who gave me a big shot of penicillin. Philip Assey had been President Roosevelt's doctor, when he had visited Bernard Baruch at Hobcaw during World War II, and was also the doctor who checked the girls' health at Sunset Lodge. I had an allergic reaction to the penicillin and ended up in Georgetown Hospital with an esophageal ulcer. After a week, I had recovered. I ended a little romance with a hospital nurse and began normal life as a fulltime resident of Pawleys Island.

---

[4] The Assey house was built in the 1930s by wealthy Mr. Metcalf. It had a flat roof and was designed to float if a hurricane lifted it off its foundation. It was on its own big piece of land, separate from the rest of the island.

PAWLEYS ISLAND

My boss at IP was Pete. He and his wife Alice lived on the mainland of Pawleys, and they introduced me to the local power structure. I already knew Linwood well enough for him to allow me to set up a fenced-in area, next to his store, and try to sell bleached driftwood that I had found in a swamp. Weeks later, a lady from Tennessee finally bought one piece before I gave up on that enterprise. I met Frank Marlow, owner of Marlow's Store, who was a good friend of Pete's and in the winter after work, we used to gather around the pot-bellied stove in his store and pitch pennies onto the concrete floor toward a wall for entertainment. If you knew Frank well enough, he would sell you a case of beer on Sunday.

Frank Marlow's Store

I also met Doc Lachicotte who, along with his father, owned the Hammock Shop. Doc invited me to become a temporary member of The Pawleys Island Episcopal Men's Club Poker Playing Society. Doc, Frank, Pete, Newt who owned the liquor store, and I occasionally met at someone's house to play poker. I would have liked to have met that beautiful blonde girl, who occasionally walked her two white poodles on the beach. I found out that she was the daughter of Joe, an Austrian who lived on the mainland and who had taught his daughter to avoid strange men. I continued to fish in the surf or from one of the bridges across the Creek, where a good catch was a quarter-pound croaker but the usual catch was an inedible catfish or dogfish. The Creek was silting in badly and had little water in it on low tide. Running out of something to do that spring, I attempted the first ever, engineless singlehanded circumnavigation of Pawleys Island. Using an inner tube, I floated from one end of the island to the other in the ocean, using a kite as a sail. Then, I paddled through the south inlet with my hands and feet and pointed my vessel north, into the twists and turns of the silting shallow creek. The voyage ended in failure against a mudbank, when my inner tube was holed by one of a condemned bed of coon oysters. I crawled up the muddy bank and onto the road with my punctured vessel and a bleeding foot.

The Lafayette Pavilion had burned down in 1957, rumored to be either the victim of a Baptist conspiracy or bad wiring. There were plans in 1959 to build a new one at the intersection of the North Causeway and the main beach road. As the spring of 1960 approached, the owners of summer homes began to come down on weekends. I was introduced to Spencer McMaster, Bill Otis Senior and Arthur Ehrich, who were all members of the Building Committee for the Pawleys Island Pavilion Association. They had most of their meetings at Spencer McMaster's beach house. They had an architect's rendering of the proposed new pavilion and they asked me to draw detailed plans that the contractor could use to build the building. The Pavilion Association was a private stock company, owned by some of the wealthiest property owners on Pawleys Island, formed for the purpose of raising money to build and operate the new pavilion. At one of the meetings, Arthur Ehrich, who was getting along in years, asked me if I would like to go fly fishing with him and his older brother on his lake near Manning. I accepted and was appointed chauffeur to drive him and his 90-year-old, retired New York doctor brother to Manning. We spent a night with Arthur's sister in Manning and the next day drove to the lake. I was given the job of boat paddler for the two old guys, while they did the fly fishing. I did enjoy their stories, although the doctor was deaf.

I finished drawing the plans for the new pavilion and a construction contract was signed with Mr. Bill Thompson, an old Scots gentleman who had done most of the building at Brookgreen Gardens and Atalaya for the Huntingtons[5] and was now almost retired. I had a chance to ask him about the tower in the middle of the courtyard at Atalaya. He said that Mr. Huntington never used plans drawn by an architect. He would take a scrap of paper, sketch out what he wanted and tell Mr. Thompson to build it. One day, he told Mr. Thompson that he wanted a Moorish tower, like one he had seen somewhere, built in the Atalaya courtyard. Thompson said he had no idea what he was talking about. Huntington made a rough sketch of how he wanted it to look, told him how big and how tall to make it, and told Mr. Thompson to have the masons lay it up out of brick. Every day, Huntington would check out how it was going and make them change a few details until it was what he wanted. He said that working for Huntington had been a real experience.

Mr. Thompson looked over my plans for the new pavilion with his superintendent and allowed that it would be no problem to finish the pavilion by July. He quickly and expertly built the 60 x 90-foot Pavilion building in time for a July 4, 1960, opening. When it came time to build booths, tables, a dance floor and the bar, I sat down with the contractor's superintendent and sketched out what I remembered from the old pavilion on a plan. One feature that was a hell of a lot better were the bathrooms, which were actual public restrooms with urinals and toilets, rather than a smelly open platform overlooking the marsh. There was a late argument among the owners about whether to name the new building "Lafayette Pavilion #2" or "Pawley Pavilion." My last contribution to construction was to letter with black paint "Pawley Pavilion" over the entrance, in two-foot high letters in German script.

I was asked to be on the Operating Committee for the new pavilion, along with Bill Collins, who was the Ford dealer for Georgetown. A young

---

[5]In 1930, wealthy Archer Huntington bought several plantations along the Waccamaw River and named them Brookgreen. His wife, Anna Hyatt, was a renowned sculptor. Brookgreen Gardens became a famous sculpture garden. Huntington also built a fireproof concrete and brick structure on the beach called Atalaya, which resembled a Moorish castle.

The New Pawley Pavilion, 1960

Pawley Pavilion, 1962

newly married couple, Lachicotte and Muff, had been hired to be the managers. They and I knew that there was no way we were going to be able to keep people from scribbling graffiti all over the woodwork, so Lachicotte, Muff and I used a book of famous quotations and a wide marker to begin the graffiti on a high intellectual plain, with quotations from Socrates and Shakespeare, lettered on interior walls over the window openings. The Grand Opening of the pavilion was a success, with a big crowd, a band, and many of the homeowners attending. The only hitch was a fight, outside, at the end of the evening, when someone hit someone else on the head with a tire tool. More outside security lighting was installed. A few of the owners seemed disillusioned by the motto of the Pavilion Association, which was "Dedicated to our Youth."

Pawley Pavilion, Dedicated to our Youth

Through another of my island neighbors, Emily, I met Tom and Mary Davis, who published *The Georgetown Times* weekly newspaper and owned a cabin on the mainland, behind Pawleys Island. The three of us became good friends and would meet on weekends at Emily's house to discuss problems of the world. Linwood Altman asked me to draw house plans for Nancy's father and mother. I did the plans and Johnny Walker, a friendly local contractor, built the house for them on a lot near Lachicotte's Store. I met Chick and Charlotte Kaminski Prevost, who owned a wonderful old beach house, which had been the Summer Academy for plantation owners' children before the Civil War.

Charlotte Kaminski's father, Joe Kaminski, was one of the sons of Heiman Kaminski, who had immigrated from Prussia before the Civil War, fought for the Confederacy, and had been influential in establishing Georgetown's shipping and hardware businesses. Chick and Charlotte moved from their house in Georgetown every year when the school year ended and stayed all summer until the yellow butterflies told Charlotte it was time to leave the beach. That June, Chick, who also worked for International Paper Company, asked me to meet his niece, who was an artist who lived and worked in New York City and was going to visit them for a week.

Chapter 5
Honeymoon on Pawleys Island, 1961

On the day I was to meet Chick's niece, I discarded my smelly mill clothes, took a shower, and put on my best Bermuda shorts and a shirt with a collar. I drove up to Chick and Charlotte's beach house and knocked on a screen door. Charlotte let me into the living room and I sat in a wicker chair, waiting for Mary. It was the first time I had been in the house. The floors were smooth, unfinished pine boards. The walls were old plaster. The beadboard ceiling was unpainted. Wood trim was painted dark green. Doors were paneled wood with old-fashioned hardware. Everything was plain and simple.

Mary appeared at a doorway and her first words were, "Would you like a beer?" I met Mary Prevost Shower in June, we fell in love and were married at Prince George Winyah, in Georgetown in December, 1960. She was a beautiful and talented girl, two years younger than me. Mary had stayed at Pawleys Island many times during her childhood, and she loved it as much as I did. She and her parents and brother first came to Pawleys when Mary was six, and they had stayed at the Seaview Inn Annex on the west side of the beach road. They came several times after Chick and Charlotte Prevost were married and stayed at the Summer Academy.

For our first date, Mary and I drove in my red MG sports car to Myrtle Beach, and I introduced her to The Bowery, a local dive, where we drank beer and danced to Turk's band. Turk played the trumpet and rang a cow bell whenever a lady customer emerged from the Rest Room. I figured that, if Mary could put up with that sort of place, she must be okay. The next night, we ate dinner at my house, HMS *Pinafore*. My mother and a friend of hers had visited me at Pawleys Island a few weeks earlier, had cringed at my kitchen facilities, and had prepared and refrigerated stacks of individually wrapped hamburger patties and portions of cooked rice, to keep her spoiled only son, Bobby, from starving. Mary and I dined on those, plus some canned peas and beer. She was impressed. During our short courtship, we waded across the creek at the south end to Debordieu Beach and discovered the half-buried ruin of an old shack on the beach. We explored Huntington Beach and walked by Atalaya, which was still occupied by the sculptor Anna Huntington. Mary sketched the historic Pawley House, Lemon House, Pelican Inn, and Summer Academy and eventually sold prints of them at the Hammock Shop.

At the end of the week, Mary and her family returned to Westport, Connecticut, and Mary started a new job in New York City. A week later, I caught the train in Florence and visited Mary in New York City, where she took me to see Three Penny Opera. That weekend we decided to get married in December, 1960.

After we were engaged, and when I wasn't working, I was restless, ready to start married life. I continued to drop in, occasionally, at the new pavilion, but I wasn't enjoying the action like I did in college. I clearly recall dancing with one of the Cassena Inn cafeteria serving girls, who told me I was the oldest man she had ever danced with, except for her daddy. I played a joke on a young friend, Bill Otis Jr., who was on vacation from college and living in his family's beach house. He had a side business, booking bands for venues along the coast. I wrote him a fictitious letter, requesting a combo for a pavilion concert, with eleven violins and a tuba. I think he took it seriously for a few minutes.

Once, on a hot Saturday afternoon in August, I visited Lachicotte and Muff at the Pavilion. There were no customers. The big empty space was cool and dark. A slight breeze blew through the propped open shutters. After a few minutes, old Mr. Arthur LaBruce pedaled his bicycle up to the pavilion entrance. He had been a fixture around Pawleys Island for many years. He slowly climbed the stairs, spoke to us briefly and sat down at the piano to play. I don't remember what classical piece he played but, for a few minutes, until he got tired and rode away, lovely sounds echoed across the empty room. Arthur and Julia LaBruce had a summer home on the mainland of Pawleys, where Arthur had an amazing collection of seashells, which he had accumulated over the years. Arthur's son became a doctor in Charleston and their daughter, Libby, was an opera singer in Europe.

During one of my walks down the beach, I saw a crowd of people gathered around. I joined the group and could see a woman in a bathing suit, lying face down in the wet sand. A man was giving her artificial respiration. I was told that an ambulance had been called but that she was probably too far gone to survive. I had never seen a drowned person before. I felt sick to my stomach and walked slowly back to my house.

When summer was over and the tourists had gone home, only we few "natives" remained. Fall and Spring were my favorite times at Pawleys Island. I moved temporarily from HMS *Pinafore* into a little beachfront house near the middle of the island. When I came home from work, if the tide was right, I would walk out toward the end of one of the groins, which were wooden walls that jutted out into the ocean from the beach and were spaced a few hundred yards apart, built after Hurricane Hazel to protect against beach erosion. I carried my baited surf casting rod and fished for drum, which fed on barnacles clinging to the groins. I found that the best time to fish was on the last hour of a rising tide. October and November seemed to be the best months, and I caught some big ones. I ate most of my night meals at the Seaview Inn.

Fishing from a Groin in Bad Weather

When November came and the time for our wedding approached, I had to find a permanent place for Mary and me to live. I had met Susie Ward, who had a tiny real estate office at the island end of the North Causeway, which eventually became the temporary Town Office. Susie was a gruff little old lady, with a bad leg, a Bryn Mawr education, and a dry sense of humor. She owned a year-round house toward the south end of the island, where she and her husband, Buck, had lived before he died. She agreed to rent her house to us until the high rent summer season began.

In November, Pete Williams and I were vote counters for the Pawleys Island precinct for the Presidential election. John Kennedy won the Pawleys Island precinct by the same small margin over Nixon that he won nationally, although I couldn't find many white residents of Pawleys Island who would admit that they had voted for Kennedy.

At the end of November, Mary quit her job in New York and moved in with Chick and Charlotte in Georgetown. Charlotte had taken charge of all preparations and events preceding the wedding. Mary and I were wined and dined by friends of Chick and Charlotte, from the beginning of December until we were married on the tenth. On one occasion we were invited to visit the beach house of Abe and Betty, who were permanent residents of Georgetown and had recently built

Charlotte Kaminski and Chick Prevost

a beach house on Pawleys Island. The house was near the beach, set well back from the road. A maritime forest hid the house from the road. We walked on a crushed oyster shell path through a tunnel of live oaks and myrtles to their house. The new house was a beautiful contemporary design with lots of glass, not like most of the houses on the island. Abe was a successful businessman in Georgetown, who owned several properties there. They and so many others of Chick and Charlotte's friends made us feel at home.

Mary's parents and brother, and my parents and several of their friends from Atlanta arrived for the wedding. The wedding was a big and beautiful event at Prince George Episcopal Church. Both of us were glad when the reception was over, and we could head south for a week alone in Florida. When Mary and I returned to Pawleys Island, we discovered that the water pipes in Susie's house were frozen solid. We had to spend that night in the old, rundown Prince George Hotel in Georgetown, where two drunks were playing a noisy basketball game in the corridor, throwing shoes into a metal waste basket.

We moved back into the beach house the next day and began to settle down. For heat, the house had a brick fireplace and one gas space heater. We had only one car, so Mary usually took me to work in Georgetown and picked me up in the afternoon. It was a big change for Mary, from working in New York City to wintertime at Pawleys Island, where there were no more than six houses occupied. Only two months before, she had been

Mary Shower & Mac in December, 1960

commuting into New York City from Westport to work in a skyscraper for McGraw Hill Publishing Company. She had friends in the City who went with her to Broadway shows and plays. She was a city girl, who missed that kind of life. Sometimes she was lonely but she was determined to make her new life a positive adventure.

The winter on Pawleys Island was beautiful. We walked on the deserted beach and threw a football back and forth. I learned that she could throw a perfect spiral at fifteen yards and lead me just right. We sat in front of a fire and talked about our lives. We had only seen each other a few times before we were married. We both had much to learn about each other. Mary had grown up on Long Island and on a suburban farm in Quakertown, Pennsylvania, outside of Philadelphia. She had gone two years to Penn State University, then, transferred to the University of Arizona. Her father, who had worked as an engineer for Bell Labs when the transistor was invented, had taken a new job in Phoenix. Mary had been president of her sorority and was an honor student. She had attended a year of graduate school at Arizona State University before moving back east to work in New York City as a commercial artist. We both knew that we wouldn't be happy, spending our whole lives in rural South Carolina. A winter on Pawleys Island was a perfect place to get acquainted but not a permanent solution to our future.

Winter, 1960

PAWLEYS ISLAND

In late January, a million menhaden crowded into the creeks behind Pawleys Island, used up all the oxygen and died. The next high tide scattered them all over the beaches, and it wasn't long before they began to stink, attracting every seagull and feral cat in Georgetown County. What they didn't eat, the tides finally washed away. That event was our biggest excitement of the winter.

Each morning, as I worked in the engineering office at International Paper Company. I waited for announcement of a promised transfer to the coast of Oregon to help manage the building of a new paper mill. Mary and I were looking forward to that new adventure. The Georgetown Mill was one of the largest paper mills in the world. For twenty-four hours a day, it turned out giant rolls of kraft paper. The mill had dominated Georgetown ever since 1937, when it was built. Half of Georgetown's population worked there. When the wind was blowing from the right direction, every Georgetown County resident had a chance to smell the stink and hear the constant roar and coded honking signals from the mill.

I thought of it as a terrible but fascinating place to work, where everything was bigger than life. I remembered the private tour that I had given McConnell a few months earlier, which he would never forget. We had walked through the wood yard, between mountains of man-sized logs, breathing a strong odor of pine resin. Hundreds of swallows swooped down to pick insects from piles of dead logs and bark. At the edge of the Sampit River, giant yellow machines roared and raked stacks of logs off steel barges, into a flume and up a conveyor, where they fell into big rotating steel drums, which rumbled and tumbled them until the bark was ripped off. Then, at the top of another conveyor, a man in a chained safety harness guided logs down a chute, into a ferocious grinding machine called a chipper, which made very loud roars as logs were reduced to little chips in one second. It was rumored that an employee had once fallen into a chipper and all they could find to bury was a finished roll of paper. From there, I guided McConnell through the lime room, where it was impossible to breathe, and up ten flights of steep steel-grated stairs to a room where wood chips were loaded into the tops of digesters, giant tanks of acid and steam that cooked the wood chips to a pulp. It was 140 degrees up there and overwhelming clouds of hot rotten egg vapors permanently attached themselves to our clothing. We didn't stay long there, but climbed down and walked across an alley to the entrance to the #1 and #2 paper machine room, where we stood between two gigantic paper machines, each one a series of huge roaring and squealing, ten-foot diameter steel rollers, over a thousand feet long. The noise they made was so loud that you thought your head would split open. All of the workers used hand signals and wore earplugs. Wood pulp was sprayed out onto vibrating steel screens at one end of the paper machine, then squeezed and pressed between a hundred giant steaming rollers. We walked the length of the room, toward the end, where 5-ton rolls of finished paper were stacked. Along the way, we watched a wide sheet of thick paper become snagged by a roller and start to rip. A siren screeched and a man with a knife ran between the spinning rollers to cut out wads of paper and stuff it into a giant hole in the floor, where the Hydropulper ground it up. I ended the tour by describing to McConnell how a man had once fallen into the Hydropulper. I offered to show him the giant sucking pumps in the basement, but he declined. When we returned to the parking lot, full of old rusty cars, McConnell's Plymouth was covered with white specks of salt cake from the mill stacks. "Uh, oh," I had said, "if we don't wash those off in the next few minutes, they will eat through your paint job." We ran his car through the free car wash that International Paper Company provided for its employees and told him to hope for the best.

Chapter 6
Building Marshmellow, 1963

In March, 1961, a recession delayed construction of the new paper mill in Oregon, and I got tired of waiting for a transfer. I took another job, which would make us move away from Pawleys Island to Wilmington, NC. Before we moved, we gave a big late winter party at Susie's beach house, to repay all of the kindnesses we had received. One Sunday afternoon, dressed up couples parked their cars at the edge of the narrow road, little ladies sank their high heels in the sandy yard and climbed the rough steps, to get to trays of dainty sandwiches and a punch bowl of "Georgetown Punch," half bourbon and half soda water, poured over a block of ice.

By 1963, after a year in Wilmington, Mary and I were living and working in Chapel Hill, NC. The year before, I had bought a $500 vacant lot on Pawleys Island, on the creek side of the dirt road that led north from the water tower. There were no houses on the marsh side of that road. The lot was located a little north of Bills Boats, a rowboat rental business. Mary and I had dreamed of owning a summer home on Pawleys Island, and we had decided to build a beach house, using our own labor, which was the only way we could afford to do it. We designed a 20- by 40-foot, one bedroom house. There was a barn in the yard of our Chapel Hill apartment, which we used to prefabricate the outside walls for the beach house. I made more than twenty 4x8 wall panels, complete with framing, siding, painting, insulation, windows, and doors.

In order to get a permit for a septic tank for the house, it was necessary to raise the elevation of the marsh with fill dirt, hauled from the mainland.

Pilings for Marshmellow

Wall Panels from Chapel Hill, 1962

Window Panels, Facing Creek

Panels and Roof Complete
after Two Weeks

Mary, Mac & Erich Unveil
Marshmellow Name

In those days, there was no law against filling the marsh, which had already been filled to create the dirt road and several other lots, east of the road. I even found an arrowhead in the dirt that was trucked from a borrow pit, west of Highway 17. Captain Vereen of Murrells Inlet, an ex-charter boat captain, was the health officer. I visited his house, and he wrote out the septic tank permit while sitting in a fishing boat fight chair, fastened to the floor of his living room.

A regular building permit for construction of the house was also required. Building permits for Pawleys Island were issued by the Magistrate Mr. Deer, who operated a store on the mainland. I told Mr. Deer where the house was to be located, filled out a form and paid fifty cents for the permit. We did have the foresight to raise the house on pilings, up eight or nine feet above the high tide level of the Creek, driven through the fill and mud into hard material. However, the pile driving contractor telephoned me in Chapel Hill after his first day's work and said that a man had driven up and told him that some of the pilings were being driven on the wrong lot. I had mistakenly located the pilings, partly on the next lot. Fortunately, I was able to buy that lot for $750. A local carpenter, Christopher Columbus Jayroe, built a structural floor on top of the piles. When we had finished building the wall panels and roof beams in the Chapel Hill barn, we had them delivered by truck to the lot on Pawleys.

Mary, her brother Ned who was working in Connecticut, and I rented a house on the mainland of Pawleys for our two-week vacations, to install the panels and dry in the roof. We carried each heavy panel up the stairs that had been built to the raised floor, set it in place along an edge of the floor, bolted it down and to each other, and braced them off, one at a time. As far as I know, it was the first prefabricated house built on Pawleys Island since before the Civil War, when rice planters prefabricated summer homes on their plantations before disassembling them and shipping them to Pawleys Island. It was tiring work and in the evening, Ned, Mary, and I would sit on a porch of the rented house, drinking beer and reminiscing about our lives.

Ned was three years older than Mary. He had enlisted in the Navy after two years of college. He had served on several ships and loved Navy life. After four years, he had returned to finish college at Johns Hopkins University, but he still didn't know what he wanted to do with his life. He was an intellectual and a thinker. He entered Yale Seminary to study to be an Episcopal minister but, after a year, quit and went back in the Navy. Serving on a ship in Europe, he had gone AWOL and tried to find a monastery to become a monk, but was persuaded to return to the ship, took his punishment, and eventually left the Navy. He was working as a graphic artist in Connecticut and was considering returning to Yale Seminary, which he did a year later. He was a hard worker, a good carpenter, and an interesting companion.

After a week we had finished installing all of the wall panels. We installed a prefabricated roof beam that ran the length of the house and set all of the roof joists, spanning from the roof beam to the tops of the wall panels. Before the two weeks were over, we had placed the plywood roof deck and nailed down heavy roofing paper to dry in the house.

During most days, we had visits from Mary's family and friends of Chick and Charlotte. Everyone seemed impressed by how fast the house took shape and how finished the outside looked, even though the style wasn't traditional Pawleys Island. Each day, we took photographs of the completed work. I must say, we were proud of our little Pawleys Island house. Mary named the house "Marshmellow" and lettered the name on a panel by the front door. The house stands today, much increased in size by other owners, from the 900 square feet that we built.

It took us another year, driving down from Chapel Hill on weekends, to complete the house. During my trips down to finish Marshmellow, I usually noticed the same group of black men sitting next to a tree along Highway 17 at the South Causeway, talking. On one trip, I needed some help with something too heavy for me to lift, so I asked one of them if they knew someone who could help me. A man, who turned out to be Mr. Harold Green, offered to help me. He was a big help to me several times after that. We did all of the work ourselves, except for subcontracting the plumbing and electrical work.

At the time Marshmellow was being built, the view from our screened porch or from the roof deck across the marsh was beautiful. There were no houses on the mainland side of the marsh. The marsh was full of life. Between the fill that was hauled in to raise the land and the brown water of the creek, spartina grass grew. Red winged blackbirds landed in the grass and made their screechy calls. Marsh hens hid in the grass and made their squawk when the sun dropped below the horizon. Purple martens darted after mosquitoes. At low tide fiddler crabs scuttled across the mud, waving their claw. Tiny creatures bubbled to the surface of the pluff mud. Clusters of oysters clung to each other and to the edge of the marsh.

During the months and years after Marshmellow was finished, both Mary's and my parents used Marshmellow and helped to complete it, as did several of our friends. We didn't get to use Marshmellow as much as we would have liked, because I took another job, and we moved even farther away to Boston for three years. Susie rented Marshmellow for us during the summers, when we weren't there. We stayed at Marshmellow during all of our vacations and had wonderful times there. Although we weren't steady church goers, each of our three sons was baptized at All Saints Church on the mainland of Pawleys Island – Robert in 1965 and Jamie in 1967 by Allan Mustard, and Charlie in 1969 by Charles Robinson.

Creek View from Marshmellow Deck

PAWLEYS ISLAND

Looking South from Marshmellow to Water Tank & Pavilion

Robert Christened at All Saints, 1964

Chapter 7
Chick & Charlotte's Summer Academy

Mary's father and mother, who had been living in Connecticut, retired to Georgetown in 1968. They bought a house near Chick and Charlotte's winter house on Prince Street. Mr. Shower was one of the first teachers at Winyah Academy, one of the private schools for white children that were started in many places in the South during the 1960s to avoid integration. He taught all of the science courses, including an oceanography course for which he wrote the textbook.

Mr. Shower had taught me to sail on his sailfish, a forerunner of the sunfish, in Long Island Sound. After they moved to Georgetown, we used to launch his sunfish into the Pawleys Island surf and sail beyond the waves. We also sailed in Winyah Bay, once sheltering from a thunderstorm under Bernard Baruch's dock at Hobcaw. He and I bought a houseboat together and explored and entertained our friends on the rivers around Georgetown. Owning that boat with him was my introduction to cruising, which eventually became the consuming activity of Mary's and my life.

Mary's family had several reunions at the Prevost-Kaminski Summer Academy. We loved to revisit that wonderful house where we had met. There was a Pawleys Island rope hammock at the southeast corner of the porch. Lying down in it after a big dinner was as near to heaven as you could get. On the west side of the house, across the paved road, was a little pier to the creek, and a gazebo where, when the sun was setting and there was enough breeze to drive away mosquitoes, Chick would bring a tray of glasses, ice and a bottle of Old Setter Bourbon, whose motto was,

Charlotte on the Beach in front of Summer Academy with a Young Friend

Leila Entertaining at Summer Academy

Sunday Family Visits at Summer Academy

Mary Introduces Robert to the Surf

Robert Getting to Know the Surf

Robert on Joggling Board at Summer Academy

Jamie and a Watermelon

"it points the way." On other occasions, the gazebo would be used to net crabs on the end of strings, baited with chicken necks. Or, at certain times of low tide, you could watch a line of black boys, walking side by side across the creek, poking the bottom with pitchforks, gigging for flounder. Before Chick and Charlotte sold the lots on either side of the house, they were thick with the trees and shrubs of a maritime forest. Oaks, myrtles, cedars, pine and yaupon covered the lots. Over the years, there were many parties on the porches of Chick and Charlotte's Pawleys Island house. Chick and Charlotte's neighbors, the Paceys, the Norburns, the Forresters, the Fogels, the Lumpkins, Fannie Brawley, Ellen Maurice, Edwin and Ethel Kaminski, all came on Sundays, after church, to sample Chick's spicy Bloody Marys and taste his "cheese things." Gladys, the cook, fixed the best shrimp pie, squash casserole, cheese grits, fried fish and peach cobbler that anyone ever tasted. After dinner, there was always someone taking a nap on the porch in the rope hammock, where there was usually a breeze. At other times during the summer, Chick and Charlotte and their friends and neighbors had parties for each other, sat on each other's porches, had a few cocktails and discussed conservative politics. Chick and Charlotte always moved from Georgetown to Pawleys before Memorial Day and moved back to Georgetown after Labor Day, or whenever Charlotte noticed the yellow butterflies heading south.

Charlotte Kaminski Prevost was an interesting woman and a force in the local social and economic scene. Her grandfather, Heiman, had been a wealthy businessman and a driving force behind any success that Georgetown, South Carolina, ever had. One of Heiman's sons, Joe, was Charlotte's father and the man who purchased the Summer Academy on Pawleys Island during the 1930s. Charlotte grew up in Georgetown and on Pawleys Island. She was an intelligent girl and earned a Masters degree from Columbia University. She taught kindergarten-aged children in her private school in Georgetown. Her family continued to own and operate a hardware store in Georgetown and owned much property in the downtown area. Charlotte's family sold some of the land where the steel mill was built in 1969. Charlotte created the Rice Museum in the clock tower. Her real love, before and after being married to Cuthbert (Chick) Prevost following World War II, was Pawleys Island and everything that went on there. They had one son, Michael Prevost. Charlotte was very kind to Mary and me and to our three sons, playing with them in the sand like another kid.

Over many years, the beach eroded in front of the house. Instead of five dunes between the house and the beach, there was less than one. The groins that were put in after Hurricane Hazel might have made erosion worse in the long run. A substantial wooden seawall was built on the beach side of the entire lot, but Hurricane Hugo took that away in 1989. Later, the beach made a small comeback, but the risk of the old brick foundations being undermined remained.

For a while, toward the end of the time Chick and Charlotte owned the Summer Academy, they occasionally entertained paying guests. I remember one story they told me about a Catholic priest who rented a room for a week and who would appear in his underwear after having too much to drink, which was most of the time. Charlotte's son Michael and Ginny were married in the Summer Academy. Charlotte died before Chick. The house was inherited by Michael and Ginny who kept it until 1986, when it was sold out of the family.

Summer Academy before Renovation

Joe Kaminski & Summer Academy, Early Days

*Young Charlotte Kaminski on
Creek Side of Summer Academy*

Summer Academy before Seawall Built

Seawall in Front of Summer Academy

Mary's 1967 Sketch of Summer Academy

Looking North from Summer Academy

Looking South from Summer Academy

I had a chance to study the details of the Kaminski-Prevost Summer Academy. It was built in the 1840s by South Carolina Governor Robert F. W. Allston, who was a wealthy rice plantation owner of several plantations along the Pee Dee and Waccamaw rivers. He was one of several planters and their families who moved away from their plantation homes every summer to avoid the danger of malaria mosquitoes and to enjoy the cool summer breezes of Pawleys Island. Governor Allston established a summer school on Pawleys Island for plantation boys, presided over by officials of All Saints Episcopal Church. After the Civil War, Governor Allston and later his wife, Elizabeth Allston Pringle, continued to grow rice on Chicora Wood plantation but eventually gave it up. The Summer Academy remained vacant for many years, until Charlotte Kaminski's father, Joseph Kaminski, bought the property in the 1930s.

I imagine that the house had been constructed by slaves on one of Allston's plantations, disassembled and transported by barge to somewhere near Hagley Landing, behind Pawleys Island. The timbers of the house had been cut, fitted, numbered, and taken apart before they were transported to Pawleys Island. The large floor timbers had been hewn from pine logs with adzes and axes, and placed on top of brick piers. The sawn floor joists had been marked with Roman numerals for identification. They were mortised and tenoned and fastened together with wooden pegs. The roof joists were similarly fastened and numbered with Roman numerals. The wall framing was fastened into the floor timbers and braced. The wooden single-hung windows had old bubbled glass. The house had withstood many hurricanes. The roof had been originally covered with hand-split cypress shingles. The exterior walls were covered with wide cypress lapped clapboards. Interior partitions were either plastered or covered with beadboard. The entire third floor, or attic space, was a dormitory for the boys. The kitchen was a separate building on the north side of the main house, connected by a breezeway. Originally, there had been no indoor plumbing, heating or electrical, and no closets. The Summer Academy was well preserved, buffered by a thick growth of trees and not ruined by modern embellishments. Like the other early houses of Pawleys Island, it represented the aura and significance of the island. The new mega mansions of the island have done a pretty sad job of destroying the original atmosphere of Pawleys Island as I first knew it.

PAWLEYS ISLAND

During the 1950s and 60s, there were no good seafood restaurants on the mainland of Pawleys Island. We would drive to Murrells Inlet and go to the Wayside, the Inlet Kitchen or Oliver's Lodge, all of which had lines of customers on weekend nights, waiting to get in. Wherever there was a Vereen running the kitchen, you could get a good fried seafood platter. Wayside was our favorite. I can remember being there with a crowd of friends and relatives, as Mary's father traded dirty jokes with Julia Kaminski, the Grand Dame of the Georgetown social scene. Morse's Oyster Roast at Murrells Inlet had good local oysters during the months ending in "r." Trays of oysters were steamed until they were ready to be opened with oyster knives. The shells were dumped through holes in the rough wooden tables into garbage cans. On the island, the Sea View Inn and the Tiptop Inn had good food, but you usually had to be staying there to be allowed to eat there. The Cassena Inn was the only cafeteria. Early on, I remember a fish house on the South Causeway and a drinking establishment at the island end of the North Causeway that sold pickled pig's feet and pickled eggs stored in gallon jars. Those establishments, the island drugstore, and the water tower eventually disappeared. Red King's Bowling Alley expanded into Funland, which had several trampolines and a putt-putt golf course before it also disappeared. We did our grocery shopping at Lachicotte's Store, run by Linwood Altman. Lachicotte's Store was not only a place to stock up with groceries for the weekend or for the entire week but also was the place to make social contact with people you hadn't realized were staying at Pawleys. Some people hung out between the rows of canned goods on Friday afternoons, waiting for someone to come into the store and invite them to a cocktail party. Frank Marlowe's store was close by and was the place to find unusual items, like rice steamers, crab traps or chicken necks for crab bait. There were other useful establishments on the mainland, like Mr. Deer's Store, the Old Post Office, the liquor store, and The Hammock Shop.

Charlotte Kaminski Prevost knew the history of Pawleys Island well and wrote the book, *Pawley's Island, A Living Legend*. I was particularly fascinated to learn the way that Pawleys Island visitors had to travel to get to the island before passable roads and bridges were built in the 1930s. If a family lived in Columbia and wanted to visit Pawleys Island, they caught a train from Columbia to Kingstree and another branch line train to the little community of Lane, where they had to spend the night in the one hotel. The next day, they caught the one scheduled train from Lane to Georgetown, then caught the *Comanche* or *William Elliott* steamboat from Georgetown to Hagley Landing on the Waccamaw River west of Pawleys Island. After the Atlantic Coast Lumber Company (ACL) train across the South Causeway was terminated in 1906, travel to the beach was by horse and buggy or early automobile. I have found rusty railway spikes on the muddy bank of the Waccamaw River at Hagley Landing. Later, car ferries and eventually, bridges spanned the Pee Dee and Waccamaw rivers. The train track from Lane to Andrews ran in a perfectly straight line. ACL used it to haul logs to their huge Georgetown lumber mill. They went out of business in 1931, and the tracks were eventually taken up and sold to the Japanese before WWII, but a perfectly straight rural road remains on top of the old railroad bed from Andrews, past the no longer existing town of Trio, to Lane.

I've driven from Columbia to Pawleys Island a thousand times since 1954, when I had my 1949 Ford convertible. With the top down, I would head east toward Sumter on Highway 76, cross the Congaree swamp, the Wateree River and an abandoned railroad track, up a hill to Stateburg, and turn right toward Wedgefield, Pinewood and Paxville. In the early days, I passed cotton and tobacco fields being plowed by farmers walking behind mules. I passed unpainted shanties, tobacco barns, and country churches. Some houses were so old and rotten that you could have pushed them over, if they hadn't already been pulled down by kudzu vines. In later days, I would stop at Harold McCleod's Store in Paxville for a beer and some redneck conversation about Carolina football or South Carolina politics. I would continue toward Manning, crossing I-95, which wasn't there until the 70s. If it was morning, I might stop at the Manning Coffee Shop. I continued toward Greeleyville, a dying town and the halfway point to Pawleys Island. One summer day, I stole a watermelon from a field between Manning and Greeleyville. It was a long way from Greeleyville to Andrews, where Joe Gibbes and I used to stop at the Ice House for another beer. If we were on our way back to Columbia and it was during early spring, we'd buy a shad roe to take home. It was eighteen miles from Andrews to Georgetown. I knew I was getting close when I smelled the paper mill. On

PAWLEYS ISLAND

one cold January night, Jim Dunbar and I were on our way back to Columbia, after giving up the idea of buying a sunken boat near Garden City for $500. We were surprised to see the dim lights of the midway of a fair, just outside of Andrews. We stopped and paid three dollars to see an old blonde stripper shiver as she danced the hoochie coochie and took off her clothes. From Georgetown, it was only eleven miles, along Highway 17 to Pawleys Island. Whenever I crossed the South Causeway and turned onto the ocean road, I felt I was in a different world, and I relaxed.

Chapter 8
Pawleys Pier Village & Belle Isle Beach House

By 1969, we were living in Columbia again. I was a project manager for McCrory Sumwalt Construction Company and in charge of building projects along the coast of South Carolina. In 1971, a group of investors bought the Pawleys Island property where the fishing pier was located. The long wooden pier had been operated as a business for many years, charging fishermen to use it. It was several hundred feet long, sticking out well into the deeper ocean where larger fish might be caught. I remember fishing from near the end and hooking something that was too huge to try to lift up to the pier deck. The other fishermen guessed that I had hooked a ray and they allowed me to work my way under their lines toward the shore. I was finally able to get to the beach with the fish still on the line. I worked it through the surf and dragged a ray that weighed more than fifty pounds up onto the beach. I didn't know what to do with it. I had heard that some people made fake scallops by cutting out parts of the wings with a cookie cutter. It was practically dead and couldn't be coaxed back to life, so I buried it in the sand.

The pier property developers planned a 9-building, 54-unit condominium project. The investors selected McCrory Sumwalt to be the contractor. One of the leading investors lived in Indianapolis and had a friend there who was an architect. This architect's design for Pawleys Pier Village looked like nothing else on Pawleys. It was as if he had never been there. We had to redesign the structures to be halfway economical and meet the local codes. Even so, the appearance of the condominium buildings was like nothing else on Pawleys Island.

There was much controversy about the project's sewage disposal system, which collected sewage from the buildings, treated it and pumped the treated effluent into the ocean at the end of the pier. Some Pawleys Island residents complained that dumping sewage or routing sewerage into the ocean at the end of the pier was unsanitary. A local health department official answered their complaints by saying that the proposed Pawleys Pier Village sewer system was much cleaner and safer than the antiquated and leaky septic tanks that Pawleys Island houses were using to dispose of their sewage. A local politician, who was also one of the investors, called me at home one night to ask me if I thought the sewer system was acceptable. He was worried how bad publicity could affect his re-election. When the project was finally approved by the County and the State, Mr. Deer, the Magistrate, sold me two building permits, one for each 6-unit building. The total cost of the permits was $20. The price for building permits had gone up a little since I bought the building permit for Marshmellow.

Our subcontractor began to drive pilings for the first two buildings, located at the north edge of the property. It wasn't long before I received an official summons from Mr. Hamby whose beachfront property was directly north of Pawleys Pier Village. I knew that he owned an old and historic house, and the driving of pilings was probably doing damage to it. I feared that Mr. Hamby, a Washington DC attorney, was not going to be an easy man with whom to deal. I slunk over and met Mr. and Mrs. Hamby, who were surprisingly calm. They had already accepted the fact that the new condominiums were going to destroy their privacy. They showed me the new cracks in the old plaster. I completely sympathized with their situation, and I think I convinced them that, like Hitler's generals, I was only carrying out orders. We agreed to fix all damage, which he accepted.

By 1971, Mary and I had sold our Marshmellow house to pay for other things, such as kids' expenses and a new house in Columbia. Because I was going to be managing construction projects along the coast during all of that year, we rented a house at Pawleys Island for the summer. It was located on the marsh, near the south end. Our three young sons loved Pawleys Island, especially building forts in the sand and trying to defend them from the waves of rising tides. They loved to visit the Prevost beach house, where Charlotte would help them collect seashells in a bucket and would sit and play with them at the edge of the surf. After a Gladys lunch, a slight sea breeze would lull them to sleep.

Little Kids, Dancing

Little Girls, Showing Off on Pawleys Island

Harriott, a friend from Columbia, and her two girls visited us for a week. The girls were close to the same ages as our boys, and they had wonderful times playing in the marsh, running around, giggling and screaming, and trying to give hair-do's to our uncooperative sons. It was a hot, sticky August. Night breezes brought in the smell of the paper mill, and mosquitoes came in around the screens. We tried closing up the house and turning on a rusty window air conditioning unit, which blew out a little cool air, but the fan blades hit the side of the metal housing and made a terrible noise. After a while, our close neighbor yelled, "Turn that damn thing off." On another occasion, a late night car careened around our corner at high speed and crashed into the thick bushes next to our house. As we peered from our window, a drunken young man with granny glasses and a cane crawled out of the car, looked up at us, said he would be back in the morning, and limped toward the north. The car stayed there for several days and disappeared one day while we were away.

When the first two condominium buildings were substantially complete, not a one of the twelve condominium units had been sold. They were listed with Doc Lachicotte, Sam McFadden, and Bumpy Thompson for prices between $54,000 and $84,000. Then, during the Easter holiday of 1972, they sold them all. The investors gave the go-ahead to build the other seven buildings and they were all sold before the completion of construction. Today, resales at Pawleys Pier Village go for over half a million dollars.

The homeowners of Pawleys Island organized to make sure that no further condominium construction ever again took place. They also politicked to have a water and sewer system installed for the whole island, doing away with treated sewage being discharged from the end of the pier and eliminating all septic tanks. The drinking water, which used to smell of sulfur and turn bourbon gray or green, became regular tasteless water.

In 1973, I became involved with a project to develop a plantation, Belle Isle, located a few miles south of Georgetown. Joe Gibbes and Mac McCrory were the other partners for the project. We became convinced that a beach house was required as an amenity to the proposed 300-unit condominium development and Pawleys Island was the closest beach, about 15 miles away. We got wind that a Georgetown attorney had a beachfront house toward the north end of Pawleys that he might sell. The property had two lots, with a house on one lot, all of which he reluctantly agreed to sell for $80,000. Our architect drew plans for a beachfront clubhouse, We located the new clubhouse well behind the primary dune. Over the years, the dune in front of the house has grown to be one of the highest at that end of the island. Once the beach house plan was approved by the County, I again entered Deer's Store and purchased a $10 building permit. Pilings were driven before other homeowners realized that the building was going to be a clubhouse. There was only one other clubhouse on the island, which was for Litchfield Plantation, and ours would be the last. A few years later, an adjacent lot to the south was bought and the new owner placed his house as close to the beach as he could. That house blocked part of our view but its foundations have been threatened by high tides ever since.

The first manager of the Belle Isle Condominiums was Ken, who had previously been manager of the Myrtle Beach Convention Center. Ken, Joe, and I drove up to the abandoned Ocean Forest Hotel at Myrtle Beach, only a few weeks before it was to be imploded. We went there to bid on and buy some silverware for Belle Isle. Ken and Ginnie lived at Belle Isle for a couple of years, before she developed a famous cross stitch kit business and their whole family moved to Pawleys Island to operate their business. We attended Ginnie's funeral at All Saints in 2011. Another friend in those days was Pete Preskof, who was a good friend of Mary's father and had a gallery on the Pawleys Island mainland for his paintings. Mary and a friend from Myrtle Beach once had a show of their own work at Pete's gallery

When the first phase of construction of our Belle Isle condominium project was completed in 1975, an Arab oil embargo and extremely high interest rates virtually stopped vacation and retirement property sales for a while. We may have been better off, financially if we had invested all of our money in Pawleys Island beach property instead of condominiums. Construction of more Belle Isle condominiums was delayed, and I was able to have myself removed from the development partnership. Mary and I continued to live in our Belle Isle condominium and to visit the Pawleys Island beach house. It was while sitting on the porch of the Belle Isle beach house in late 1975 that Mary and I talked about what to do with our lives, now that I had no job. We agreed that it was time for some big change, an adventure that would bring our family close together and show us that we could accomplish something by ourselves. We made the decision to take what money we had left, look for a sailboat, take the boys out of school, and live on the boat in the Bahamas.

We found an acceptable boat in a marina in Southport, North Carolina. It was an old wooden sailboat, a two-masted ketch thirty-eight feet long, big enough for the five of us to live on. It was a classic design by a well-known naval architect, William Atkin. It was double-ended with a long bowsprit. The keel had been layed in a boatyard in Texas before the start of World War II but it wasn't launched until 1946. The boat had had several owners but had spent most of its life in the Carolinas. The present owner was a young man who was willing to sell it for a reasonable price. It looked like it had been well cared for but the auxiliary engine had been removed and was supposed to be rebuilt. We bought the boat, and I began to make trips to Southport to work on it, awaiting delivery of the rebuilt engine, so we could motor it back to Georgetown. Because it was such a heavy and sturdy looking boat that would demand a lot of attention, Mary decided to name her *Matriarch*.

By the end of 1975, the rebuilt engine had still not arrived. We decided to have *Matriarch* towed down the Intracoastal Waterway a hundred miles to the marina at Belle Isle. Mary's father drove Robert, who was eleven, and me to *Matriarch* on the last day of the year to meet an old fisherman in a Harkers Island fishing boat, who was to tow us to Georgetown. It was a two-day journey with a number of groundings and mishaps, but the old fisherman dropped *Matriarch* off at Belle Isle Marina and returned to Southport, insisting on motoring all night in the ocean rather than repeating the ICW route.

I bought a new diesel engine in Charleston and helped a mechanic install it. Mary and I worked every day to prepare *Matriarch* to leave Georgetown. The other teachers at her school and most of our friends thought we were crazy to plan such a trip but we were determined to do it. On Valentine's Day, 1976, we said goodbye to all of our children's classmates and their parents and motored out of Belle Isle Marina, headed south down the ICW.

The boys, Robert 11, Jamie 9, and Charlie 6, were excited and enthusiastic about the trip from the very beginning. It was crowded below deck and cold in the cockpit but we managed to establish a routine. The boat had an adequate galley with a propane stove and an ice box, a head with a marine toilet, and bunks to sleep on, although they were narrow. We didn't try to put up any sails, partly because the channels were too narrow and partly because we didn't know how to sail such a big boat. Our only experiences with sailing had been on sunfish sailboats. We went aground several times in this big boat with a six-foot draft, and we had to wait for a higher tide to get underway again. We had previously arranged to stop at a marina in Melbourne, Florida, for a few weeks to complete some maintenance and hopefully learn how to put up the sails and navigate the boat.

Mary had brought some of the books from the school where she had been teaching, and we began to try to establish some regular educational instruction. Most of the useful things that the boys learned were from nature around us and from maintenance of the boat. As we learned how to put up sails, tie off lines, steer with the tiller, use the compass, and pull up the anchor, they learned the same things and did most of them equally as well as Mary and me. Other sailors in and around the marina were helpful to us, and we were able to leave and head south again with more confidence than before.

We stopped in Miami for a few days but moved farther south to Biscayne Key to await good weather to cross the Gulf Stream to the Bahamas. A cold front kept us anchored for a few more days. On Easter morning we motored out of Hurricane Hole, put up the mainsail, jib, staysail and mizzen, and motorsailed fifty-five miles to Gun Cay in the Bahamas, arriving in the mid-afternoon. That short voyage, out of sight of land for the first time, was a big first step toward learning to feel comfortable cruising long distances, day and night. Mary and I felt proud that we had been able to do it. We cleared Customs and continued toward Nassau.

We motored across the shallow Great Bahama Bank, avoiding many ugly yellow coral heads. A day later we approached busy Nassau Harbor after nightfall. The lights of automobiles crisscrossed the harbor and made it impossible to see the two weak range lights that led into the harbor past shallow rocks on either side of the narrow channel. We finally made out the range, entered the dark harbor, and anchored for the night. The next morning the boys woke us, saying we were surrounded by giant cruise ships and we were blocking the turning basin. We hastily relocated *Matriarch* to a marina on Paradise Island.

After a few days in Nassau, we continued toward the Exuma Islands. Unable to identify the island within sight, we anchored, studied the charts and finally figured out that the island was Highborne Cay. We worked our way down the Exuma Cays past Normans Cay to Staniel Cay, where we tied up at the Happy People Marina. By this time each of us had routines and chores. Robert and Jamie dived down to retrieve conch shells from the bottom, which were opened and the meat prepared in one of several ways. Jamie climbed coconut palm trees and tossed coconuts down to be opened for the milk and meat. Charlie had a regular chore of pouring buckets of salt water on *Matriarch*'s wooden deck, which would shrink and leak despite all of the work I had done to recaulk it. As we sailed from island to island, the boys made friends with kids on other boats and with native kids on the shore. At Staniel Cay, we ate dinner in the Royal Entertainer Lounge, where Mrs. Rolle served up conch fritters or hamburgers. A nearby table of German sports fishermen took an interest in our boys, bought them ice cream, and lectured them on remaining close friends all through life. Before we left Staniel Cay, the boys discovered an islet cave, which had been used in the James Bond movie, *Thunderball*. There was a hole in the top which Jamie dropped through into the water below, much to our horror when we found out later.

Our southernmost destination was George Town on Exuma Island. We anchored in front of the Peace and Plenty Hotel. In backing up to set the anchor, I heard a crunch from the engine compartment and the engine ran no more. The mechanic and I hadn't aligned the engine shaft properly and the transmission housing had cracked. I ordered a replacement transmission from Florida, which was supposed to be delivered to the little airport in George Town. I rode my little fold-up bicycle a couple of miles each day, expecting the part from Florida but it was a week before it arrived. Meanwhile, we sailed across George Town Harbor to Stocking Island, which had a good beach for the boys to explore. Also, Jamie saved a little redheaded girl from drowning in the Peace and Plenty Hotel swimming pool, but her mother didn't even thank him. The boys were encouraged to draw and color pictures of the things they saw, and it was during this trip that Charlie showed his talent for art that continued throughout his life.

After installing the new transmission, we started back toward the north, visiting Governors Harbor and Hatchet Bay, Eleuthera. Hatchet Bay was the headquarters for a big live chicken business, and the boys made it their business to run alongside a corrugated tin building full of chickens raking sticks on the tin siding that disturbed the chickens into full squawks. The dockmaster at the marina there took the boys fishing, caught fish and showed them how to gut, skin, and fillet a fish. All during the trip, the boys trolled lines from the stern and often caught fish. There was a little yacht club at Hatchet Bay where we met other sailors and watched old movies that were shown outside.

We anchored at Spanish Wells where Mary celebrated her fortieth birthday. A fisherman's wife made her a purple cake. We anchored at Great Stirrup Cay and toured the lighthouse. We noticed a big cruise ship on the other side of the island. We walked over to where jolly boats from the ship were ferrying passengers ashore for lectures and a barbeque. A midwestern couple spied us, standing under some palm trees, and they thought we were characters out of the book, *Swiss Family Robinson*. We were surrounded by admirers of our tans and bleached hair. We also received a free meal.

On July 25 we made our first long overnight voyage, which was from Great Stirrup Cay to West End, Grand Bahama Island. That was our last stop in the Bahamas. We made another overnight voyage from West End to Cape Canaveral, Florida. From there we motored several days up the ICW to Fernandina Beach, where we decided to take one more overnight voyage to Charleston. During that night the wind behind us increased to twenty-five to thirty knots. Water from the following sea flooded through the exhaust pipe and ended use of the engine. The mainsail became stuck behind the spreaders, and I couldn't reduce the area of the mainsail, so we turned back downwind and scooted along at more than eight knots. In early morning we identified a buoy off Kiawah Island and, by early afternoon we were off the jettied entrance to Charleston Harbor. As we made the turn to go in under sail, a Polaris nuclear submarine roared out between the jetties and forced us to get out of the way. I didn't think we had wind from the correct direction to sail up the channel, and I suggested to Mary that maybe we should seek a tow from the Coast Guard. That suggestion did not sit well with her, and she ordered me to put up all sails and she would steer. Robert helped me as I slid out onto the bowsprit to raise the jib. Mary steered between the jetties, and we heeled over with the sails pulled in tight. She steered straight up the channel until the wind died, just in front of the Charleston Coast Guard Station, where we anchored for the night. The next morning I flushed the salt water out of the engine with oil, and we motored back to Belle Isle Marina, arriving on August 4, 1976.

PAWLEYS ISLAND

Soon after we returned from the Bahamas, I was offered a job in Greece and we lived there for two years. When we returned to South Carolina, we bought a house in Mt. Pleasant and I started a Construction Management business in Charleston. For the next twenty years, our visits to Pawleys Island were limited to family reunions at the Summer Academy. During those twenty years, Chick and Charlotte and many of their friends died. The Pawley Pavilion had burned down under mysterious circumstances and hadn't been replaced.

At the time of Hurricane Hugo, September 1989, Mary and I were still living in Mt. Pleasant. We had our share of damage to our own house and our boat from the hurricane and didn't have a chance to visit Pawleys Island until more than a month later. As we drove north from Mt. Pleasant, almost all of the pine trees along Highway 17 were broken off, about a third of their height above the ground and were laid over in the direction that the wind had blown them. Awendaw and McClellanville were disasters. When we approached Georgetown, the wind damage didn't look too bad, and we thought that perhaps Pawleys Island had been spared. When we crossed the South Causeway, we could see that the damage was not so much from the wind as from the tidal surge. What dunes that were there before the storm were washed away, as were several of the houses.

We approached the Summer Academy with trepidation. Chick and Charlotte Prevost had both died previously, and the Summer Academy had been sold outside the Kaminski-Prevost family. When we drove into the yard of the house, it was a sad sight. The sand dune in front of the house was gone. The separate kitchen building had been totally destroyed by the surge from Hugo. The front third of the main house was gone. I looked past the blue tarps into the plastered living room where Mary and I had first met. The living room was a wreck but most of the back half of the house was intact. We hoped that the new owners would have the desire and the resources to restore it. Chick and Charlotte used to have framed *New Yorker* magazine covers hanging from the old wooden walls, and we found a couple of them lying in the sand. The only object we found and took away was a wooden timber, which had been part of the stem of the river steamboat, *Comanche*. I had cut it from the wreck of the riverboat on the shore of Goat Island and given it to Charlotte, years ago. She used to ride on the

Comanche from Georgetown to Hagley as a child, before the first bridges were built across the Waccamaw River. We didn't think that the new owners would mind our taking it.

Summer Academy after Hugo

Hurricane Hugo, 1989

Chapter 9
Growing Old

In 1998, we moved back from Mt. Pleasant to the same condominium at Belle Isle that we had first owned in 1974. Our sons were grown and had their own families, but some of their toys were still on the shelves of their bedroom. The Belle Isle beach house at Pawleys Island was still there, although it had been damaged by Hurricane Hugo in 1989. The apartment under the house, where we used to stay, had been washed away and hadn't been replaced. After building Marshmellow, Pawleys Pier Village, the Belle Isle beach house, and a few other Pawleys Island projects, I stopped building things on Pawleys Island, except for a small addition to Wynken, Blynken and Nod, and a house on the mainland near the Hammock Shop for an old high school friend. Mary and I were content to walk the beach or rock on the porch of the Belle Isle Beach House with a G&T, remembering past times at Pawleys Island.

Many things looked the same in 1999 as they had in 1974. The waves and sounds of the surf were the same. Seagulls still soared and screeched. Lines of pelicans still glided low along the beach. Sandpipers ran in the wet sand where sand fleas and periwinkles burrowed. Ghost crabs dug homes in the dry sand. Empty seashells still lay at the edge of the surf at high and low tides. Starfish, jellyfish, and horseshoe crab shells still washed up on the beach. In the salt marshes along the creek, fiddlers still backed away and waved their claws. Blue crabs in the creek still grabbed hold of chicken necks on the end of strings, minnows wiggled in the shallows, and mullet jumped. Children still built castles in the sand with moats and watched them wash away at high tide. Boys and girls still waited for the right wave to body surf toward shore, scraping their stomachs on the sandy bottom. Fishermen fished from the same pier or stood on the beach and cast their weights beyond the surf, waiting for a jerk on their baited hooks. Old people wore hats and walked barefoot at the edge of the surf, some with heads down, looking for their favorite shells. Girls and boys lay on beach towels, soaking up the sun, or built sand castles or played football or frisbee or volleyball or bocce, marking out boundaries in the sand. Most of the historic houses remained. The little white church still had weddings and worship services. The Hammock Shop still sold rope hammocks.

I have always liked to walk along the Pawleys Island beach in winter, when north winds blew, waves were high and even when cold rains soaked everything. I wore layers of warm clothes and rain gear, leaning into the wind as I trudged along. The waves and rainy wind sounds brought back memories of long ago sailing adventures on our boat, *Rocinante*, sailing down the Caribbean Thorny Path to Venezuela and back in 1988 and sailing across the Atlantic to Europe after repairs from Hugo were completed. Mary, Robert, Jamie, and I made the long passages from Charleston to Cornwall, England in 1991. Mary and I had sailed alone in Ireland and France during the next two years; and all four of us sailed back across the Atlantic from the Canary Islands through the Caribbean to Charleston in 1994. (These adventures were chronicled in my prior memoir *Cruising Through Life*.)

We had learned to endure rough cold weather and to complete all passages that we started. I remembered one time when Mary and I were sailing alone at night from Ireland toward Falmouth, England, in a gale in the Celtic Sea. We had missed our chance to sail around Lizard Point and would have to hole up in the port of Newlyn. We were headed there, passing Seven Stones Lightship and Bishop's Rock Light, which protected boats from running onto the rocks of the Scilly Isles. I could barely see the conical peak in Mounts Bay ahead in the distance. I was steering and Mary was below, exhausted and asleep. I thought to myself at that moment, as gusts of wind drove waves across the cockpit, rain poured down my collar, and I fought the wheel and gripped the helmsman's seat with my knees, "What would happen if I get too tired to keep on doing this, or what if I have a cramp or pull a muscle, or what if my cap shrinks around my head and I faint, or what if the wind keeps picking up and I have to go forward to shorten sail, or a shroud parts, or the mainsail rips?" None of those things happened and by noon, we were safely in the port of Newlyn. As we tied up to other boats that had weathered the storm, I got the same feeling of relief that I got every time I crossed the bridge onto Pawleys Island.

As we move well into the twenty-first century, Pawleys Island remains one of the only strictly residential private barrier islands in South Carolina that can be accessed by road. There have been changes at Pawleys Island, compared with when I was there in the 1950s and 1960s. The new houses along the beach are generally larger and uglier, with a lot more glass. The water tower is gone. The last pavilion burned down and was not replaced. More surfers on boards wait beyond the waves near the pier for the right ones to come along. Wind surfers, kayaks and Hobie Cats are seen off-shore or pulled up on the beach. Sunbathers wear hats and use sunscreen. A town government was formed and Bill Otis was forever mayor. The wooden groins protruding from the beach have been strengthened with stones. The North and South Causeway bridges are wider and built of concrete. Dogs are on leashes. There is hardly a lot left on the island that hasn't been built on. There are many more restaurants and stores on the mainland and traffic is much heavier. More residential developments near Pawleys Island have sprung up east and west of the highway, vastly increasing the number of people using Pawleys Island, especially in the summer. Parking cars on the island has become a real problem. The post office has been replaced. Lachicotte's Store has been renamed. Marlow's Store has been turned into an elegant restaurant. Utility lines are being put underground and a new Town Hall built.

Although the beach, the surf, the shells, the birds, and beautiful views of the ocean are still there for us to enjoy, some of the beachfront has eroded and many of the sand dunes have disappeared. High tides are getting higher and higher, eating away the dunes that protect the island. Renourishment of beach sand by pumping it from offshore has become an ongoing and expensive necessity. Sometimes, I wonder how much longer the houses on this barrier island will withstand the tides and storms of the future.

2017 was the last year that Mary visited Pawleys Island. Tragically, she was diagnosed with cancer that year and passed away in April, 2018, just two months after our youngest son, Charlie, was killed in an accident in Charleston. Soon after Mary's death, many of our family and friends celebrated Mary's and Charlie's full and happy lives at a wonderful event at the Belle Isle beach house on Pawleys Island. I still visit the Island, walk the beach, sit on the porch, and cherish the memories of my love story.

The End

Mary and Mac aboard *Exodus* at the 2014 Georgetown Wooden Boat Show. *Exodus* won prizes in 2010 and 2013 for being the most beautiful sailboat.

Appendix
Remembering Boats

Approaching eighty years old, Mary and I continued to visit Pawleys Island, sitting in rocking chairs on the porch, looking at the ocean's glitter and reminiscing about our sailboat adventures, especially our latest one. It began as a result of a mistake during the winter of 2009, when we were already well into our seventy's. It occurred less than a year after we had sold a canal barge, which we had owned and cruised on the French canals for twelve summers. We'd owned all sorts of boats – sailfish, sunfish, runabouts, houseboats, old wooden sailboats, cruising fiberglass sailboats, an old Dutch canal barge, and a steel trawler. It hadn't been a business for profit, either, because we had lost money almost every time we had sold a boat. It was a mental condition which had become permanent. Like many other cruising couples we had graduated from small sailboats to larger sailboats, made long distance ocean passages and cruises until age began to impose limitations, sold the sailboat, bought a comfortable trawler, sold the trawler, bought the canal barge in France, and sold it in 2008, thinking we had done it all.

However, our sons had inherited some of our same obsessions and one of them kept e-mailing me photographs and write-ups of used cruising sailboats that he had found, wandering through the Internet, boats that were for sale for sixty or seventy thousand dollars. I kept telling him to stop sending me that stuff. I couldn't afford to be involved with any more sailboats. I had already done that and was too old and poor to repeat it. I told him he ought to aim smaller and cheaper and work his way up, as he could afford it. To give him an example, I googled up the website of Wooden Boat magazine's on-line display of used boats, hoping to find something he might be able to afford. There were some pretty hopeless cases in the under twenty thousand dollar category, fixer uppers that would cost much more to restore than the original cost of the boat. And then I saw her, *Exodus*, what an appropriate name, a thirty-foot double-ended, gaff-rigged full keel wooden cutter for sale on Long Island Sound for fifteen thousand dollars. There had to be something wrong. She was too beautiful. I was hooked again. I was no longer thinking of a boat for my son. I had to have it for Mary and me. To make a long story short, I corresponded with the owner of *Exodus*, flew up to New York in February, believed his story that the engine would run, that she was in sail away condition and that there were others with checks, waiting in the wings, and I bought her then and there.

Mary agreed she was beautiful. My son Jamie and his family agreed she was beautiful. I had a few second thoughts but the deal was done, and I had to figure out what we had to do to sail *Exodus* from Long Island Sound to Georgetown, South Carolina, during that summer. I started making lists, my favorite pastime, making lists and buying things. I spent hours in Boaters World's going-out-of-business sale and in West Marine. Packages came from Defender Industries and Jamestown Supply. I dug through the attic for old charts of Chesapeake Bay and the coast of New Jersey. The screened porch began to fill up with stuff, all to be put aboard *Exodus*.

I decided to drive the loaded van to Mt. Sinai, NY, where *Exodus* was located. Mary didn't believe all of the stuff would fit into the van, so I had to prove it, a week ahead of leaving. The van was down in the stern but it was all in there, including Jamie's family's camping gear. The plan was for Mary and Jamie's family to take the Amtrak to Grand Central and the Long Island Railroad to Port Jefferson in June. I would meet them, Mary would get on board *Exodus* and Jamie would drive Leigh and the three children to New England to camp out for their vacation. I arrived at the Old Man's Boatyard in Mt. Sinai on May 18 and was met by Pete, the previous owner of *Exodus*. The next day he started the engine, pulled away from the mooring and backed into a boatyard slip, where I could start unloading stuff from the van. Pete was an indispensable help in familiarizing me with the peculiarities of *Exodus*.

Exodus had an interesting history. She was designed by William Garden, a well-known naval architect on the west coast. His book, *Yacht Designs*, included the Bull Frog, which was the design of *Exodus*. The boat was thirty feet long, plus a five-foot bowsprit. She had a beam of ten feet, drew five and a half feet, and displaced eight tons. She was double-ended and was steered by a tiller. She had a gaff-rigged mainsail, a boomed staysail, and a jib. *Exodus* was built in Tacoma, Washington, in 1962 by William Deaton, who gave her the name. He built her for himself with closely spaced oak frames and heavy Alaska cedar beams and planking. He intended to live aboard with his wife at retirement. However, she became ill before they could cruise on *Exodus*, and he sold the boat in the late 60s. The new owner (someone named Sid) sailed her through the Panama Canal and along the coast of South America, eventually living aboard her in Florida. *Exodus* was sold again and moved to Long Island Sound, where she had lived for the last thirty years.

Pete, the previous owner for fifteen years, was a skilled cabinetmaker and had maintained and improved *Exodus* during the time he owned her. He told me that he had done about eighty per cent of what he wanted to do to *Exodus*. He had replaced many of the galvanized fasteners with stainless steel, replaced several planks, rebuilt the trunk cabin, replaced the bulwark, reconfigured the main cabin, fabricated a new boom, gaff and bowsprit, reworked the four-cylinder diesel, and refinished the mast and all other bright work. I think he had run out of gas with *Exodus*, his sailing partner had died, and he had obtained another and larger project boat to work on.

The drawbacks of *Exodus* included no head, no pressure water or water storage, only one battery, an old diesel engine, old sails, no lifelines or pulpit, no canvas dodger, no anchor windlass, no refrigeration, and no dinghy. The good parts included a hull and decks that didn't leak, a good bilge pump, a new alcohol stove, a good depth finder, sails with no holes, and an engine that sounded okay. For the next month I worked to stow away everything necessary for Mary and me to live aboard. I temporarily eliminated two of the four berths, using the space for storage. I bought a dinghy and outboard engine, a cooler, water storage containers, fuel jerricans, an extra battery, a boarding ladder, an extra anchor, an awning, and the all-important wag bag temporary toilet that stowed completely out of sight.

Pete and I replaced a worn out jib halyard and installed a pair of used jib sheet winches. I installed a stern light and got the compass light working.

When Mary arrived on June 13, *Exodus* was about as ready as I could get her. Mary approved of most things I had done although she did rearrange a few things. I was certainly ready to get away from Old Man's Boatyard. The boatyard had no shower and no hot water. May and June set a new record for rain and cold weather. I had finally gotten used to cold sponge baths and to crawling, lifting and bending, and had even retrieved two dead pigeons from the very back of the bilge. Robbie, the crusty old dockmaster had been nice enough to allow me to stay at the dock rather that making me move *Exodus* back to a mooring. I had met several very friendly sailors. Among them, Gene, a man of 73 who had worked for 22 years to build a beautiful wooden Al Mason double-ender from the keel up. Gene custom designed and built every detail of the boat. His boat was chocked up in the boatyard, as it had been for most of its life, and Gene came almost every day to attend to some detail. He had done everything except cruise it, and he told me he was a little sad to see his dream finished.

Before Mary and I left Mt. Sinai, we met a retired couple who owned a sailboat on a mooring near us. She invited us to their house, picked us up, took us shopping, allowed us to take showers and do laundry at their beautiful home, fed us a delightful dinner, gave us a bag of goodies for later and took us back to *Exodus*. They knew what sailors far from home want and need, they expected nothing in return, and they only wanted to share sea stories with us.

Without ever having sailed a gaff-rigged sailboat, Mary and I left Mt. Sinai on June 25 on a windless day, motoring east toward Mattituck Creek. We had decided to spend a month in Long Island Sound before heading south toward home. We had never sailed there. Our only experience near there was when we had bought our Hans Christian 38 cutter in Kennebunkport, Maine, in 1987 and had sailed outside from Point Judith, Rhode Island, to Norfolk. Pete said goodbye to us, saying he expected us to have our greatest summer yet, sailing *Exodus* in Long Island Sound.

We stayed a couple of miles offshore, navigating to waypoints plugged into Garmin's most basic GPS and using 1985 paper charts that I had bought when we owned a trawler. We entered Mattituck Creek, motored three miles to its end and were anchored by 2 PM, after a passage of about 25 miles. We stayed in Mattituck Creek for a couple of days; then headed farther east through Plum Gut toward Shelter Island. About four miles from Greenport, the engine quit. I had no idea what went wrong or how to fix it. We put up the main and jib in very light air and made almost no progress. I knew I should have joined Sea Tow, but I hadn't. I called them. They asked if I was a member. I said no, but I'd like to join that moment. No, they said, this tow is going to cost $325/hour. The tow boat showed up awhile later and *Exodus* was towed to the fuel dock at Brewers Sterling Harbor in Greenport.

The next morning I requisitioned a mechanic, whom I knew would be very expensive. While waiting, I decided to try one desperate fix. The only fuel tank was a bladder tank in the lazarette, which was supposed to hold eighteen gallons. I topped up the bladder tank from the jerricans, which took ten gallons to fill. I checked the yellowed dog-eared Isuzu engine manual and saw that there was a hand-operated fuel pump. I found the pump and operated it, watching fuel rise in the glass bowl. I turned on the ignition, operated the glow plug, and pressed the starter. The engine started right up without missing a beat. I had done a dumb thing, run out of fuel. I cancelled the mechanic, and we moved to a marina slip. I joined Sea Tow by telephone.

While still at Greenport, a man in another boat looked across the top of a shed roof and noticed the distinctive wooden mast of the gaff-rigged *Exodus*. It couldn't be, he thought, but he decided to check anyway. Bob and his wife, Nancy recognized *Exodus*, which he had owned for twelve years. I had previously talked with him by telephone, and he had given me much of the early history of *Exodus*. We had a reunion aboard *Exodus*, the boat on which he lived when he met his wife. We arranged to take a sail the next day, accompanied by another old sailor who had been a crew member of *Exodus* when she encountered a storm off the coast of Maryland in 1988. We had a great time with them. Bob gave me an old chart which showed a previous *Exodus* owner's location on Christmas Day, 1969, in Colombia, South America. He also gave me a copy of the written account of a storm experience aboard *Exodus* and some photographs of *Exodus* when she was still registered in Oregon, and when she still had a head. After the sail we took a mooring at Dering Harbor on Shelter Island, and Bob and the rest of the crew took the ferry back to Greenport.

While at Dering Harbor, I made a list of a typical routine aboard *Exodus* while at anchor, as follows: Empty pee pots, fill kettle, light stove for coffee, wash face, dig out granola bars and instant coffee, turn on VHF for weather report and Yacht Boy radio for National Public Radio news, take down anchor light, drink coffee, set up wag bag toilet, use wag bag toilet and put it away, wash dishes from last night, fill small water containers from large one, brush teeth, plan next passage and put waypoints in GPS, check oil, check fuel tank, pump rain water out of dinghy, wait for fog to lift, crank engine, raise anchor, get underway.

Our next destination was Three Mile Harbor, on the south fork of Long Island, near East Hampton. We had been given instructions by a friend as to how to find a particular mooring. Being mostly a land person from NYC, he had instructed us to turn right between two white posts and go about seven long blocks to a white ball with someone's name on it. We finally found it, tied on, and motored our dinghy about three-quarter of a mile to shore, where we were met by our friends, Tim and Maureen. For the next three days we stayed at their home, ate their food, drank their whiskey, were entertained by them and their friends, and had a wonderful time. On the fourth of July we tried to take a group of seven for a sail, but for the first time the wind blew over twenty knots, and we decided not to put up the sails. Instead we motored and partied, which was probably the wisest plan. After three days we felt ourselves getting soft, so we made an early departure across Long Island Sound to the Connecticut River. We caught the current through Plum Gut just right, made good time and rode up the River on an incoming tide, past Essex to the beautiful and popular Hamburg Cove. We took one of many moorings in a basin surrounded by trees and hills, topped by substantial homes.

While in Hamburg Cove, a sailor from another boat dinghied over and became acquainted. Elliot asked our itinerary and we told him it was our intent to work our way west toward NYC, go through the City and tie up at the 79th Street Boat Basin on the Hudson River, so we could visit the City on Mary's birthday, July 17. He recommended a better alternative. His homeport was Mamaroneck, NY, only nine miles from NYC. He said it would be easier to moor there and take a train to the City than to fight the current up the Hudson River. We thanked him and decided to take his advice.

After a day and night in Hamburg Cove, we returned downstream to Essex and rented a mooring there. The price of a mooring included launch service to and from shore, which was very convenient. Essex proved to be a lovely town. We ate at the historic Griswald Inn and visited the Connecticut River Museum.

At each stop along the way we pursued sources of block ice, water, fuel, groceries, New York Times, places to charge the cellphone, showers, and laundromats. Usually, most of these essential items could be found somewhere within walking distance or by finding a ride with someone. So far, we hadn't run out of anything nor had we gone hungry.

On July 10 we motored out of the Connecticut River and headed west, a mile off the Connecticut shore. A convenient anchorage was at the Gulf behind Charles Island near Milford. We anchored close in to uninhabited Charles Island, listened to the birds in the trees, some strange ones making funny clacking noises and others sighing like babies. Mary saw a deer, and there were probably other creatures living on the island. The next day we crossed Long Island Sound to wide open Huntington Bay. Our destination was Northport, a long way into the Bay. It was a Saturday and every boat was out, roaring around with big wakes. The passage into Huntington was narrow and crowded. We hadn't expected so many boats. When we called Seymour Boatyard, which advertised 500 transient boat moorings, we were told they were full. They recommended we call Centerport Yacht Club, which we did and they assigned us one of their few remaining moorings. We found it, but before night fell the owner of the mooring returned and we had to take another mooring. On Sunday many boats left, and we were told to move, once again. There was launch service to shore, where we found all of the basic essentials, including The Godfather sandwich at an Italian deli.

On July 14 we crossed Long Island Sound once again, to the north side. The Sound was much narrower here and it was a short passage to Mamaroneck. We were headed toward a buoy that was supposed to mark the outer entrance into Larchmont and Mamaroneck but as Mary strained to make out the buoy, she could see only a cloud of tiny sails, as kids in Optimist sailing dinghies tacked back and forth. Larchmont has a reputation as a sailing center with summer camps and schools training kids to be future sailboat racers.

We often found that the most difficult part of a passage is approaching a harbor or anchorage for the first time. This summer, almost every harbor was new to us, so we scanned the chart and shoreline for clues as to exactly where we were. As usual, when we were a little closer a red buoy became visible among the forest of little sails, and we could identify our position and which way to go to enter Mamaroneck. We followed the buoys into the harbor and approached an empty space at a pier at Orienta Yacht Club. We spotted the sailboat of Elliot, the man who had recommended Mamaroneck, and we were greeted by a club member who introduced us to this friendly and informal place. They assigned us to an offshore pontoon, which was very convenient and close to shore. Another transient sailboat, owned by an Italian who ran a restaurant in Greenwich Village, occupied the other side of the pontoon. He was on vacation and entertained other Italian friends by cooking aboard his boat until late at night. The Club provided launch service to shore. We could walk four or five blocks along the main street to the New Haven railroad station, which was only thirty-five minutes from Grand Central Station.

We traveled by train to NYC three days in a row. The first day we spent at the splendid Morgan Library and its recent beautiful addition, viewing very interesting exhibits of manuscripts, sketches, music, letters, and seals. We ate a wonderful dinner at the Chez Napoleon Restaurant, which had been recommended by our friend Tim. The next day we spent at the Frank Lloyd Wright exhibit at the Guggenheim. It was Mary's birthday, and we splurged by each having two Manhattans at the Oak Room of the Plaza Hotel, total cost $100. The third day we had excellent seats for the matinee of *South Pacific* at Lincoln Center.

The next part of our trip would be the most hazardous of the summer. There is no inshore way for a deep draft sailboat to take a protected route past the coast of New Jersey. From Sandy Hook to Cape May, about 110 miles it would be necessary to sail in the ocean. We have made many offshore and overnight passages on other sailboats, but I had uneasy feelings about this passage. I've always been a worrier, and I was finding myself becoming more anxious about passages like this. I anticipated problems, most of which probably wouldn't occur. Once we were underway, I always put those fears behind me. I think I've gotten worse as I've grown older. I wish I could face each new day with eager and positive anticipation.

The weather report for July 19 was favorable, as was the timing of the tidal current past Hell Gate and through New York City. We got underway at 0615, accomplished the nine miles past Execution Rock in less than two hours, and were hurtling down the East River at more than seven knots. There was some turbulence and a few navigational uncertainties but everything went smoothly. Mary took many fine photographs as we passed under eight major bridges and past the skyscrapers and landmarks of the City. By the time we reached the Statue of Liberty and Governors Island, it was only noon, so we decided to skip Sandy Hook and head out of the Ambrose Channel and into the Atlantic. We rolled in the wakes of several big ships and tugs towing barges. There was an unfavorable wind causing a chop that slowed us down. We had considered going all night to make Cape May the next day. However, we reached Manasquan Inlet just before dark and, because of the chop and a possible need for more fuel, we decided to go in. Once inside, we had no place to tie up. We spotted an open space in front of a crowded and noisy restaurant, so we pulled in and tied up. A wedding reception was going on and the bride and groom were herded in front of *Exodus* for a photograph. Despite the noise and confusion, we were so tired we collapsed. After midnight there was a knock on the side of the boat and a man told us we couldn't stay there. I told him we had boat trouble, and he said we could wait until the next day to be towed away.

Early the following morning I was up at 0500, carrying the jerricans in search of fuel. Manasquan has a big commercial fishing fleet, which was unloading twenty-four hours a day. The manager wouldn't sell me any fuel because I wasn't on a commercial boat. He did tell me where to buy fuel, and we moved *Exodus* to the fuel pier. The weather was deteriorating, so we decided to find a marina near Manasquan. We called Brielle Marina Basin, which had space. We were told to motor past a bascule railroad bridge, which stayed open except when a train came, turn right past the bridge and someone would show us which slip to take. We made it past the bridge against a three-knot current, turned right and saw a man pointing toward the worst open slip that I could imagine. We had to do a 180-degree turn and go with the current into the slip, somehow stopping before we rammed the fixed pier. Miraculously, we turned around without hitting anything and Mary tossed a line to the man on the pier. He managed to stop us but the current was too strong for him to pull us against the pier. He eventually called for help and the two of them pulled *Exodus* to the pier.

The railroad bridge, only a hundred yards away, opened and shut 25 or 30 times a day to let trains pass. A bridge siren sounded, the bridge gears ground down, the train whistled, the bridge siren sounded, and the gears ground up. Other than those noises, the marina was pleasant. The town had little of interest beside restaurants. We had signed up for three nights, thinking it would take that long for the weather to clear up. On the second day I watched a 70-foot yacht get swept against the bridge and wedged there. Tow Boat US showed up with three boats, hooked lines onto the yacht and waited until the tide turned to pull the yacht off.

After the second night the weather turned for the better, and we left the next morning on a slack tide. We cleared Manasquan Inlet into the Atlantic and headed south toward Cape May. There was a favorable wind, so we put up the sails, shutting down the engine for the first time. By this time we knew how long we could motor before adding fuel to the bladder tank. We transferred fuel with a siphon pump from a jerrican, when we figured we had used five gallons. By nightfall we were nearing Atlantic City. It took forever to pass the lit up skyscrapers, some changing color every few seconds, for effect. We still had 35 miles to go to reach Cape May. We motorsailed through the night, reaching the hard-to-see jetties of Cape May by dawn. A wicked current tried to push us toward the rocks. We doused the sails and motored our way between the jetties. Once inside, we followed the red and green buoys until we approached a dredge working in the channel. We thought we were taking a route to clear the dredge, but men started screaming at us and chased us down in their workboat. They said we were headed toward the dredge pipe, so with some difficulty we followed them through a narrow gap next to the dredge's cutter head. We had selected Utsch's Marina and found it at 5:30 AM. We headed diagonally toward their entrance and watched the depth sounder drop from nine feet to five feet before we reached the entrance. We tied up to a pier and waited for the staff to arrive. Finally, we were assigned a transient slip and were treated very well. They had the best showers of the trip. We slept well, glad that that section of the trip was over.

While we were there, another Charleston sailor visited. He had a big and fancy 55-footer with a 75-foot mast, meaning he couldn't get under the bridges of the ICW and had to go everywhere, outside. He planned to have his boat shipped to the Virgin Islands for the winter. He suggested that we might be able to rent his slip in Mt. Pleasant.

We enjoyed the town of Cape May with its Victorian houses and pedestrian street. We re-provisioned there and on July 25 picked a rising tide to go through the Cape May Canal and up Delaware Bay toward the Chesapeake. The distance was too far to go in one day, so we decided to anchor in the Cohansey River on the New Jersey side of the bay. The river was very deep and had a swift current, so we continued up the river to a place where marinas showed on the chart. It was a Saturday and several sailors saw us and beckoned us into a vacant space. We headed into the current and, with their help tied up to a floating pier. When I shut down the engine, I heard water running into the bilge. It didn't take long to realize that the sea water pump was leaking badly. I shut the seacock and took the pump out and apart. The bearings and seals were shot, and we were lucky to be where we were. There was a mechanic nearby who could order and install the parts. The marina owner and the sailors there were very friendly and made us feel at home. Because we had planned an intermediate stop to avoid hurricane season in South Carolina, we decided to leave *Exodus* there for a month or so. On July 28 we were given a ride to the Amtrak station in Wilmington, Delaware, and caught the overnight train to Charleston. We were back at Belle Isle by midday on July 29.

It didn't take long for me to become restless in Georgetown and want to return to *Exodus*. On August 25 Jamie drove me to the Charleston Amtrak station, and I rode the overnight coach to Wilmington, where I was met and driven to Hancock Harbor Marina, where *Exodus* was tied up on the inside of a long floating pier. I moved aboard, saw that the water pump had not yet been replaced and was assured by telephone that the pump was there and would be installed very soon, which it was. I settled into a solitary routine, doing a little sanding, scraping and priming, waiting out the days until Jamie would join me to make the next leg of the trip south. There was very little activity around the marina during weekdays and, without a car I was restricted to walking around the marina and looking at the interesting boats tied up to piers and blocked up in the boatyard. I watched the Travelift dangle a beautiful Bristol 47 sailboat above the river, while the owner lowered an eight-foot centerboard to apply bottom paint. I watched a boatyard crew plaster another layer of fiberglass over the hull of a sturdy Westsail 42. I was offered a ride to the little community of Greenwich, a beautiful collection of old wood, brick and stone homes, several from Pre-Revolutionary days. This part of New Jersey is very rural, full of soybean fields and large tree nurseries.

Warm days and cool nights came and went with a little rain, but generally much more pleasant than August and September in coastal South Carolina. I called Mary almost every evening to learn what was happening around Belle Isle and with the rest of our family. Jamie was to take a week off to help me move *Exodus* through Delaware Bay and into the Chesapeake. He arrived on Amtrak on September 5, two days before Labor Day. There was a sailing regatta and two big parties at the marina during that weekend, so we didn't sail out of the Cohansey River and into Delaware Bay until Monday, September 7. Fortunately, the river current was with us and a rising tide carried us up Delaware Bay. As we entered the 14-mile long Delaware-Chesapeake Canal, the current changed in our favor. We motored at six to seven knots and entered the northern Chesapeake in early afternoon. Many boats of all types were out on The Bay on this Labor Day. There was enough of a favorable breeze to put up all three sails. We passed Bohemia Bay and the Sassafras River, rounded Worton Point and anchored in Worton Creek at 1900. We had come 55 nautical miles and deserved a couple of rums and some peanut butter crackers before lighting the anchor light and turning in.

The next day was nice, but worse weather was predicted to be on the way. We sailed down Chesapeake Bay to Annapolis and through a narrow opening bridge over Spa Creek to a beautiful calm anchorage. Jamie went ashore in the dinghy to tour the old Maryland State House and bring some ice back to *Exodus*. On the following morning the weather was still good enough to travel, so we got underway after the 0900 opening of the bridge, headed for Oxford on the eastern shore. The wind was 15-20 knots on our beam, and we made good time under sail toward the Choptank River. When we turned up the wide river in mid-afternoon, we were headed directly into a 25-knot wind, with gusts to 30. Jamie doused the sails and we motored against steep swells. *Exodus* hobbyhorsed, with the bow crashing down and the propeller sometimes revving up as it rose out of the water. We were making only two knots up the river, when a larger sailboat approached from the opposite direction under a scrap of sail, swooshing past, toward I know not where. It was tempting to follow him but Jamie convinced me to continue bashing toward Oxford. Finally, we turned into the Tred Avon River. By the time we reached Oxford, the water was calm enough for little radio-controlled model boats to race in front of the Oxford Yacht Club. There were many marinas to choose from at Oxford, and we called Campbell's Boatyard and were assigned a slip, just at closing time.

Our intention was to reach the southern Chesapeake by the end of the week, when Jamie would have to go back to work. However, the weather continued to deteriorate and blew up a gale, so we stayed in Oxford, which wasn't a bad place to be stuck. We bicycled through the beautiful old town, past classic boatyards and boat builders to The Schooner for beer, bar food and football on TV. Mary drove up to take Jamie's place, and Mary and I stayed one night in the classic Robert Morris Inn. Jamie drove back to Charleston on Sunday, September 13.

Mary and I got underway the same day, along with more than 100 other sailboats, returning to Annapolis after a big weekend race. It was a beautiful day and we sailed most of the way to Solomon, Maryland, where we anchored for the night. We left early the next morning for a long motor trip across the mouth of the Potomac River and into the Wicomico River to Reedville. The entrance to Reedville was flanked by many nets and fish traps, which were tricky to avoid. We followed one of the big old trawlers of the last Virginia menhaden fleet into Reedville, where we anchored close to the fish processing plant, hopefully upwind of it. The noise from its grinders and machinery went on all night but we slept in spite of the noise.

We awoke to an odor that was like being inside of a cat food can, and we quickly upped anchor and got underway. We pushed south across the mouths of the Rappahannock and Piankatank rivers to Mobjack Bay and into the Severn River, and tied up at the end of a pier at the Severn River Marina. This was our destination for leaving *Exodus* until mid-October, the usual end of hurricane season in South Carolina. Fellow cruisers had told us about this friendly marina, where a number of liveaboards spent summers before heading south for the winter.

While there, *Exodus* was lifted out of the water by a Travelift and transported to the boatyard for painting the bottom. It was the first time we had seen *Exodus* out of the water, and we were pleased to see how true and sturdy were her lines. Youngest son Charlie drove our van up from Georgetown and helped us paint the bottom. *Exodus* went back in the water on Monday, September 21, and into a slip to wait for a further move south. Mary, Charlie, and I returned to South Carolina.

On October 10, Mary and I drove a rental car back to Severn River Marina, intending to get underway the next day. However, bad weather followed us, and we were delayed by high winds and cold rain until October 20, when we headed for Norfolk. By this time every other snowbird boat had decided to head south, so we were accompanied by dozens, if not hundreds of other boats. We anchored in the Lafayette River, across from Norfolk Yacht Club. The next morning's temperature was in the forty's, and I had a more difficult time starting the old Isuzu diesel. Once underway, we passed the remaining piers of parked ships and began a process of waiting for the openings of rush hour restricted bridges. We finally entered the ICW ditch, which would dominate the rest of our trip to South Carolina.

Exodus could motor only forty or fifty miles during these shorter fall days, and there was no convenient anchorage between Great Bridge, Virginia, and Coinjock, NC. There was a defunct and abandoned marina at Pungo Ferry, and we tied up to its derelict pier. However, the wakes of passing power boats tried to slam *Exodus* against a wall, so we pushed farther into the old marina and managed to turn a protected corner, where there was barely six feet of water. I worried that the tide might fall and leave us high and dry but was relieved to read in a cruising guide that this section of the ICW is not affected by tide.

We left early the next morning and made it to a familiar anchorage in the Broad River, just north of Albemarle Sound. There, we were treated to one of the most beautiful sunsets of the trip which Mary successfully photographed. We also encountered thousands of mosquitoes, which we battled to their death. Afterwards, Mary probed in the darkness of a cabinet under the alcohol stove for the right pot to cook dinner. In another dank locker she found the right can and in a third locker the spices. She poured water from a plastic jug, lit a burner, and cooked up a gourmet delight. After dinner we poured more water in a plastic dishpan, washed, rinsed and dried the dishes, and dumped the dirty water overboard. By then it was time to retire.

On October 23, we crossed Albemarle Sound and stopped at Alligator River Marina, a pleasant place with a basic restaurant and very nice showers. We met a naval architect from another sailboat who admired *Exodus* and who knew *Exodus'* designer, William Garden, personally. He took photographs of *Exodus*, and we each wrote a letter to William Garden, who is over ninety years old and lives on an island in western Canada.

We were advised by a local fisherman with a beautiful wooden boat to delay another day, when the wind would shift from south to north and we would have better days to cross Pamlico Sound and run down the Neuse River. We made our next run to Dowry Creek Marina near Belhaven. The wind did shift, and we got underway on a chilly nasty morning with mist and drizzle. In the dim morning light we huddled in our open cockpit with no dodger, wearing our yellow foul weather jackets and pants. We were cold and soon soaked through. I steered with the tiller, and Mary picked out distant navigation markers along the wide and choppy Neuse River, using binoculars and a paper Waterway chart inside a plastic envelope. The old Isuzu engine roared and clacked, seemingly content to run forever. The ports and hatches were closed, the dropboards in, and the decks soaked by rain. The jib and staysail were tied down but flapped in the wind as we bounced along. The rain stopped in the afternoon and we made it into Orienta Marina. I shut down the engine and prepared for the next day's run. I topped up the oil because there is a leak somewhere that ends up in the oil pan. I checked the engine belt, which is wearing away and needs constant pampering and adjustment. I topped up the main fuel tank from a diesel jerrican, using a siphon pump. I dared not let the main tank get low enough to suck air, as it had once in Long Island Sound. I checked the battery voltage, praying that the glow plugs would work the next morning and the starter would kick off the old Isuzu.

On October 27 we arrived at Morehead City, tying up at the very nice Morehead City Yacht Basin, which was full of "big dog" sports fishing boats. I watched an 82-footer take on 2500 gallons of diesel. The dockmaster said it burned 150 gallons an hour. On October 29 we arrived at Swan Point Marina but missed a turn and ran aground in their entrance. I finally managed to back out of the mud, turning much of the engine cooling water to steam and making me fearful that the whole trip was over. However, she cooled down, and we were on our way again the next day.

October 30 was a lousy, misty day, all day. It was a day of waiting for bridges to open. As we sat in our open cockpit, we watched and were watched by dozens of other boats, all waiting for the same bridge to open. In addition to palatial motor yachts, sports fishermen and trawlers, all of which would roar by us with various levels of civility in their wakes, there were many other sailboats. Most of them were in the 40- to 45-foot category. None of them could have masts over 65 feet high, because of the height of the ICW fixed bridges. We saw no other boats built of trees or gaff- rigged or steered by tiller. They were all stamped out of fiberglass or metal, mostly with sleek racy designs, but some trying for an old-fashioned look, with bowsprits, cosmetic teak do-dads or windows in their transoms. Without exception, their cockpits were completely enclosed by canvas and plastic, protecting the steersman from bad weather and keeping moisture away from all of their sensitive electronic gear – computer screens that showed exactly where they were, GPS's, autopilots, radars, radios, cellphones, televisions, sound systems, gauges, sensors and controls which made life on their boats more comfortable. Their sails were roller furling, controlled from their enclosed cockpits. They were dry and we were wet. Why weren't they out in the ocean, battling their way south, instead of motoring down the ICW? They were equipped to be out there. Some might say that this is an age of ostentatious ships and timid men. Of course, we weren't out in the ocean either, but we had more reasons not to be. I think most of the other boats looked on us as some kind of nuts from the past, either too crazy or too poor to join the modern yachting fraternity. They might be right. Some of them appreciated the lines and beauty of *Exodus* and a few probably admired what we were doing.

We made our 40 or 50 miles a day, stopping at Masonboro Boat Yard, Southport Marina and a marina just before the Little River Swing Bridge. There, a commercial fisherman admired *Exodus* and told us he thought we could make it all the way to Georgetown on the next day's tidal currents, rising from Little River Inlet and falling toward Winyah Bay. On November 2 we got underway at 0700, passed Hagley Landing at Pawleys Island at noon and were tied up in Georgetown, South Carolina, at 1600. Our voyage, which started in Long Island Sound in May, was over. It was the most special and satisfying voyage of our boating careers, partly because, although *Exodus* and her crew might be old and slow, we had reached our destination without damage, in good health, and with renewed love and respect for our boat and for each other.

The End

About the Author – Robert (Mac) McAlister is a retired construction manager and sailor, who has previously written the sailing memoir, *Cruising Through Life*, and four South Carolina non-fiction maritime history books, *Wooden Ships on Winyah Bay*, *The Life and Times of Georgetown Sea Captain Abram Jones Slocum*, *The Lumber Boom of Coastal South Carolina*, and *Georgetown's North Island*. He lives in Georgetown, South Carolina.

www.ingramcontent.com/pod-product-compliance
Lightning Source LLC
Chambersburg PA
CBHW051637120626
46551CB00014B/2117